Early Lufkin Texas

From An African American Perspective

By
Ron Price

Copyright @2022 by Ron Price

Early Lufkin
Table of Contents

Table of Contents iv

List of Figures vi

List of Tables xi

Preface xii

Introduction xvi

1 Montana – At the Start 1

2 Sawmills 7

3 Welcome to Lufkin 13

4 The Architect 21

5 Daily Routine 29

6 Lufkin Land 45

7 Nazi Camps in Lufkin 49

8 Black Wall Street 53

9 Cornerstone Employers 87

10 Churches 95

11 Grade Schools 107

12 High Schools 113

13 Cotton Club 147

14 Hallowed Ground 157

15 Montana Folklore 165

Appendix 1 – Family Tree 179

Appendix 2 – Texas History 183

Notes 189

Bibliography References 195

Figures and Tables Bibliography 201

Author's Page 217

Index 219

List of Figures

Fig. 1. Rev. Betty Kennedy, c. 2015 xii

Fig. 2. Diboll History Center xiv

Fig. 3. Montana Lillie, c. 1965 1

Fig. 4 Emma and Montana, c. 1952 3

Fig. 5. Map of Camp Creek, LA...4

Fig. 6. Map of Sabine Parrish, LA 5

Fig. 7. Lumbering in Southwest La., c. 1937 8

Fig. 8. Logs hauled by Fisher Sawmill commissary. 9

Fig. 9. African American floating logs at sawmill...................10

Fig. 10. LA. Lumber Boom, c.1880- 1925. 11

Fig. 11. Typical sawmill worker houses in Bogalusa, La. 12

Fig. 12. Great Southern Lumber Mill in Bogalusa, La. 12

Fig. 13. African American Mosaic 13

Fig. 14. H.E.& W. Texas RR Depot in Lufkin, c. 1907. 14

Fig. 15. City of Lufkin, c. 1930 - 1960s 17

Fig. 16. First Street, c. 1940. 18

Fig. 17. First Street, c. 2006. 18

Fig. 18. Angelina Four, c. 1940..19

Fig. 19. Negro Sharecropper...20

Fig. 20. Angelina Hardwood Lumber Co., c. 1930s.................23

Fig. 21. Black Historic District, c. 1930s – c. 1950s.................24

Fig. 22. Brookshire Brothers, c. 1921. 26

Fig. 23. Harry Abram, c. 1960. 27

Fig. 24. "Shotgun" houses on Chestnut St., c. 1950. 30

Fig. 25. Third Ward Houston shotgun houses, c. 1970..........31

Fig. 26. Lufkin, Texas - Downtown c. 1930s - 1950s..............34

Fig. 27. Fire Station and City Hall, c. 1902. 36

Fig. 28. Black men working on the rail. 37

Fig. 29. Jim Crow mandated segregation. 38

Fig. 30. Downtown, c. 1950. 39

Fig. 31. Pullman porter on the train. 40

Fig. 32 Negro Brakeman 41

Fig. 33. Dr. Percy Simond, c. 1955. 43

Fig. 34, Site of former Lufkin Land & Lumber Company. 45
Fig. 35. Typical East Texas Sawmill, c. 1910. 46
Fig. 36. Ties awaiting creosote treatment.............................47
Fig. 37. Lufkin, Texas - Lufkin Land, c. 1930s-1960s 48
Fig. 38. Former POW Camp in Lufkin.................................50
Fig. 39. WWII soldiers with captured Nazi flag, 1945............51
Fig. 40. "Rothammer", Former POW Camp in Lufkin 52
Fig. 41. Negro Beauty Shops, c. 1956. 55
Fig. 42. Smith Beauty Shop, c. 1956. 56
Fig. 43. Houston Tatum Cleaners, c. 1956............................57
Fig. 44. Haircutting In Front of General Store, c. 1939...........57
Fig. 45. Local Negro Businesses, c. 1956. 58
Fig. 46. The Lynne Theatre, c. 1940s. 59
Fig. 47. Pines Theatre in Lufkin, Texas, c. 1940. 59
Fig. 48. Tims Funeral Home, c. 1956...................................60
Fig. 49. Lewis Service Station & Malone Barbershop 61
Fig. 50. Colonial Mortuary, c. 1956. 62
Fig. 51. Finus Price, First Negro Blacksmith, c.1960. 63
Fig. 52, Typical Blacksmith Shop, c. 1910s...........................64
Fig. 53. Typical cotton gin, c. 1940s....................................64
Fig. 54. Lufkin, Texas – Downtown, c. 1930s-1960s...............65
Fig. 55. Angelina Hotel & Coffee Shop, c. 1920s. 67
Fig. 56. King Faisal II touring a cotton gin plant, c. 1952.......68
Fig. 57. Lufkin, Texas - North Addition, c. 1930s-1960s. 69
Fig. 58. Charlie Williams Yankees, c. 1956...........................72
Fig. 59. Lewis Motel & Beauty Shop, c. 1956. 73
Fig. 60. Carl Williams Yankees, c. 1956................................74
Fig. 61. James Hackney Grocery Store, c. 1956. 75
Fig. 62. James Hackney, c. 1956. 76
Fig. 63. Typical East Texas Diner c. 1940s............................76
Fig. 64. Dr. Samuel C. Packer, c. 1956. 77
Fig. 65. Sheppard's BBQ, Est. in 1955 by G.S. Sheppard. 78
Fig. 66. Martin's Dental Clinic..79
Fig. 67. Ida V. Givens, Agent, Atlanta Life Ins.. c. 1956 79
Fig. 68. House's Cafe, Est. 1943, c. 1956. 80
Fig. 69. William & Son Grocery, Est. 1937............................81

Fig. 70. East Tx Undertaking, Est. 1926. 81
Fig. 71. Inez Tims, Influential Local Leader, c. 1956. 82
Fig. 72. Slim Jenkins' Garage, Est. 1948. 83
Fig. 73, Gulf Service Station, Est. 1954. 83
Fig. 74. Geneva's Drive-In, c. 1956. 84
Fig. 75. Universal Life Ins., A.H. Carlton, c. 1964. 84
Fig. 76, Lufkin Foundry, c. 1956. 87
Fig. 77. Texas Foundry, c. 1956. 89
Fig. 78. Texas Foundry Employees, c. 1956. 91
Fig. 79. Texas Foundry Negro Employees, c. 1955. 92
Fig. 80. Southland Paper Mills, c. 1956. 92
Fig. 81. New Zion Baptist Church, c. 1920s. 95
Fig. 82. New Zion Baptist Church, c. 1940s. 96
Fig. 83. Goodwill Baptist Church, original, c. 1900. 97
Fig. 84. Goodwill Baptist Church (new), c. 1921 97
Fig. 85. First Baptist Church, c. 1912. 98
Fig. 86. Mt. Calvary Baptist Church 99
Fig. 87. Shiloh Baptist Church 100
Fig. 88. Long Chapel C.M.E. Church, c. 1946. 101
Fig. 89. West End of God in Christ. 102
Fig. 90. Other Lufkin Area Negro Churches. 103
Fig. 91. Other Negro Churches. 104
Fig. 92. Lufkin, Texas, c. 1930s - 1960s. 105
Fig. 93. G.W. Carver Elementary 107
Fig. 94. First Graders Carver Elementary, c. 1956. 108
Fig. 95. Olivia R. Hackney Principal 109
Fig. 96. Brandon Elementary School 109
Fig. 97. Original Melinda Garret Elementary School 110
Fig. 98. Melinda Garrett 110
Fig. 99. Third Grade, c. 1956 111
Fig. 100. Newer Garrett Elementary School 112
Fig. 101. Cedar Grove Elementary 112
Fig. 102. Lucky Ward School, c. 1920-1923 114
Fig. 103. Lucky Ward Graduating Class, c. 1920s 115
Fig. 104. Lucky Ward Faculty, c. 1920s. 116
Fig. 105. Dunbar High School, c.1924. 118

Fig. 106. William Brandon, c. 1956...119
Fig. 107. Dunbar High School Faculty, c. 1934. 121
Fig. 108. F.W. Thomas Dunbar Principal, 1943-44. 123
Fig. 109. W.R. Smith, Dunbar Football Head Coach 125
Fig. 110. Dunbar District Champions, 1943-44....................126
Fig. 111. Dunbar Football Team, 1939 127
Fig. 112. Dunbar Pep Squad Leaders, 1943-44...................128
Fig. 113. Typical Flatbed Truck, c.1930...............................129
Fig. 114. Dunbar Basketball Team of 1938...........................129
Fig. 115. Dunbar Leadership, 1943-44..................................130
Fig. 116. Miss Dunbar, 1943-44 131
Fig. 117. Dunbar High School Band, c.1956.........................132
Fig. 118. English Departments., c. 1964. 133
Fig. 119. M.E.Lyons Dunbar Principal, 1959-1968...............134
Fig. 120. Student Safety Patrol, c.1956. 134
Fig. 121. New Dunbar High School, c. 1952.........................135
Fig. 122. Dunbar Football Coaching Staff, 1964. 136
Fig. 123. 1930 Track Team 137
Fig. 124. Varsity Football Team, 1964. 138
Fig. 125. Dunbar Tennis Team, 1964. 139
Fig. 126. Girls' Track Team, 1964...140
Fig. 127. Girls' Track Team...140
Fig. 128. Dunbar Domestic Engineers, 1964........................141
Fig. 129, Miss Dunbar, 1964. 142
Fig. 130. Lufkin Dunbar Jr. High 143
Fig. 131. Dunbar Library 143
Fig. 132. Lufkin, Texas - North Addition 144
Fig. 133. Square Deal Taxi Stand, c.1956.............................147
Fig. 134. Dancing in a Zoot Suit, c. 1944.............................150
Fig. 135. Ray Charles Fig. 136. Little Richard 151
Fig. 137. B.B. King 152
Fig. 138. Duke Ellington 152
Fig. 139. Fats Domino 153
Fig. 140. T. Bone Walker...153
Fig. 141. Sammy Davis Jr.   Fig. 142. Ike and Tina Turner154
Fig. 143. Ethel Waters, c.1943 154

Fig. 144. Otis Redding 155
Fig. 145. Lufkin, Texas - Historic District 157
Fig. 146. Montana Lillie Home, c. 2006 159
Fig. 147. Lucky Ward Deeded Plat 161
Fig. 148. Typical Country Outhouse of the Period 162
Fig. 149. Galvanized Metal Washtub 163
Fig. 150. 428/430 Chestnut, c. 1970 165
Fig. 151. One Mule and the Land 166
Fig. 152. Doing Laundry with a Scrub Board & Tub 166
Fig. 153. Churning Butter 170
Fig. 154. 1956 Studebaker 174
Fig. 155. Montana Lillie Grave Site 176
Fig. 156. Emma Lillie Grave Site 176
Fig. 157. The White Dove as a Messenger of the Dead 177
Fig. 158. Emma Lillie, c. 1950s 179
Fig. 159. Bobby Jindal 180
Fig. 160. L.C. Lillie, c. 1970s. 180
Fig. 161. Patricia Lillie McKenzie, c. 1960s 181
Fig. 162. Clark Jackson Price, c. 1948. 182
Fig. 163. Vera Lillie Price, c. 1940s 182
Fig. 164. Lorenzo de Zavala 184
Fig. 165. Major Henry Wynkoop Raquet 187

List of Tables

Table 1. Sites for Black Historic District 25
Table 2. Site locations Lufkin Downtown 36
Table 3. Site locations for Lufkin Land. 48
Table 4. Site locations for North Addition 71
Table 5. Site Locations for North Addition...................146
Table 6. Title History for 428_429 Deed 160

Preface

"We are a people that have been lost in the history books of our time and for many years there were no readings, no writings of our people and to have living history records in forms of tapes and videos it certainly makes it important for our people to know about our people."

– Rev. Bettie Ruth Engram Kennedy

Fig. 1. Rev. Betty Kennedy, c. 2015
Lufkin Daily News

This book was a journey of personal discovery for the author. It began as my grandfather's life story and conveying how such an ordinary person deserved his story to be told. Now, the book turned into a tribute to all the African American men and women in Lufkin in the 1930s through 1960s. They had to face the daily challenges of the past while still steadfastly building for the future. In the end, this is a story of how an entire generation paved the way in this small East Texas town in the early to mid-twentieth century for others to follow. In other words, this is their legacy. Unfortunately, their story is largely untold. This strange disappearance of an entire population of a small town is probably not due to some sinister plot to ignore Negroes; it seemed more the consequence of the white press and business leadership more focused on big industry and influential leaders. It was as if they didn't matter and thus rendered them invisible while in plain sight.

As with any story based on decades-old recollections from numerous individuals, facts are sometimes merged, displaced and contradictory. Consequently, their experiences have been pieced together from many sources, including interviews conducted by the **Diboll History Center**. With the sole objective to dutifully re-tell their story, this book has been stitched together so that those who follow will not forget them.

It is the solemn responsibility of any historical non-fiction author to retell past events as accurately and fairly as possible. We must give a voice to those who have passed and can no longer tell their own story. In doing so, the author must speak as they would speak. Consequently, the frequent use of "Negro" describes African American people and institutions in the 1930s - 1960s. During this time in United States history, the reader should understand that the term "Negro" is commonly used and "colored" less frequently in the African American community, e.g., Negro College Fund, Negro Baseball League, and National Association of Colored People.

This inclusion was not meant to be derogatory or divisive. Those period words are included in this book in the pursuit of authenticity. Just as any reputable author would not have a jet plane reference in a story set in 1875 or call a buddy their "BFF" for a story set in 1920, this story must be faithful to the times. - Author

Special Thanks to the Diboll History Center in Diboll, Texas. Without them, this book would have been infinitely more challenging to write.

Fig. 2. Diboll History Center
@2022 Google Maps Data

Introduction

Montana McKinney Lillie, affectionately called the "Mountain Man" by his grandchildren, was not a remarkable human being. He was not a celebrity or history maker. He lived a hardworking life in somewhat anonymity. However, those who knew him well found his life inspirational. It is the basis of what has allowed the African-American community in Lufkin to survive, thrive, and take their rightful place in American success.

Through Montana Lillie and his contemporaries' eyes, this book will allow the reader to experience what it was like living as a black in Lufkin, Texas, from the 1930s to the 1960s. His life closely mimics the lives of so many other African Americans in the early days of the 20th century. Many early African American pioneers who settled in Lufkin were not born there. There were no governmental support programs or "social safety nets." they came mainly searching for jobs and opportunities with a strong willingness to work.

These pages will allow the reader to follow Montana's journey from the Louisiana sawmills to the early days of Lufkin. Read as he and others built a solid foundation for future generations. We now call them ancestors; he called them friends and family.

Thanks to the **Diboll Historical Center**, which interviewed contemporary African Americans, capturing their experiences and recollections of early Lufkin. Much like the *Slave Narratives,* where we get a peek, if not fractured remembrance, of a moment in time that helped shape this country, these interviews are an honest attempt to capture life as it was, good, bad, happy and sad.

1
Montana – At the Start

On January 8, 1901, Montana was born to Allen and Georgia Sweet Lillie in Many, Louisiana. *(For some unknown reason, Montana later changed his family name from "Lilly" to "Lillie.")* Life in those times in that part of the world was not easy for the former slaves and their offspring.

Fig. 3. Montana Lillie, c. 1965
(Author's family photograph)

Sabine Parish was the southern neighbor of Natchitoches Parish, one of the country's most highly dense plantation areas. By the end of the Civil war, the Natchitoches landscape was dotted with cotton and sugar cane plantations. Its leading citizens were frequently plantation owners and others whose livelihood depended on these centers of commerce.[1]

The early records for Montana provided a roadmap of his striving to provide for his young family. He secured one job after another. This accomplishment was not trivial for an American African with a 4th-grade education.

Montana only completed the 4th grade in Many. Emma finished the 6th. In 1910 less than 2% of the state's black youths between 15 and 19 years old were enrolled in high school.[2]

Montana Lillie's life was very similar to the ordeals and joys of many early Black Americans. Life held the promise of the American dream – own property, decide what you want to do in life, enjoy the fruits of your labor, care for your family and ensure that they and future generations find life fulfilling and happy. Unfortunately, the promise and the reality must have seemed far apart to him.

This book is a story of a generation with little formal education and meager funds that set out to claim their future. Montana joined other African Americans to own homes, build churches and stand atop a family tree that produced lawyers, bankers, engineers, fathers and mothers. He accomplished most of these acts from a homestead predated the Republic of Texas.

Fig. 4 Emma and Montana, c. 1952
(Author's family photograph)

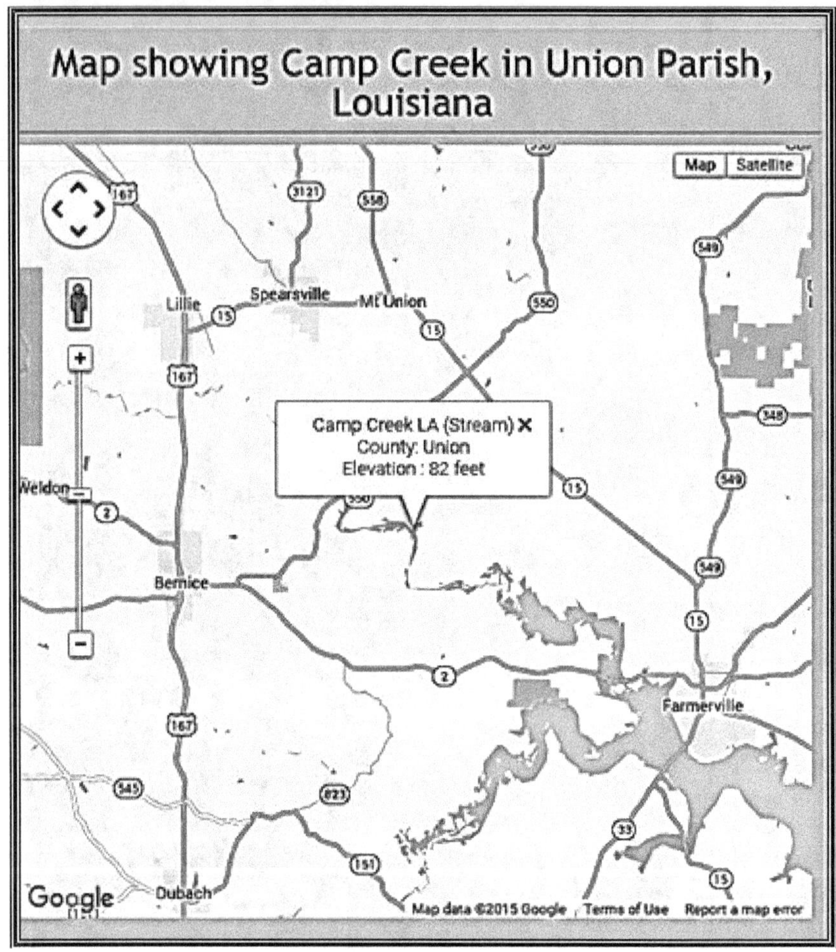

Fig. 5. Map of Camp Creek, LA
Hometown Locator.com

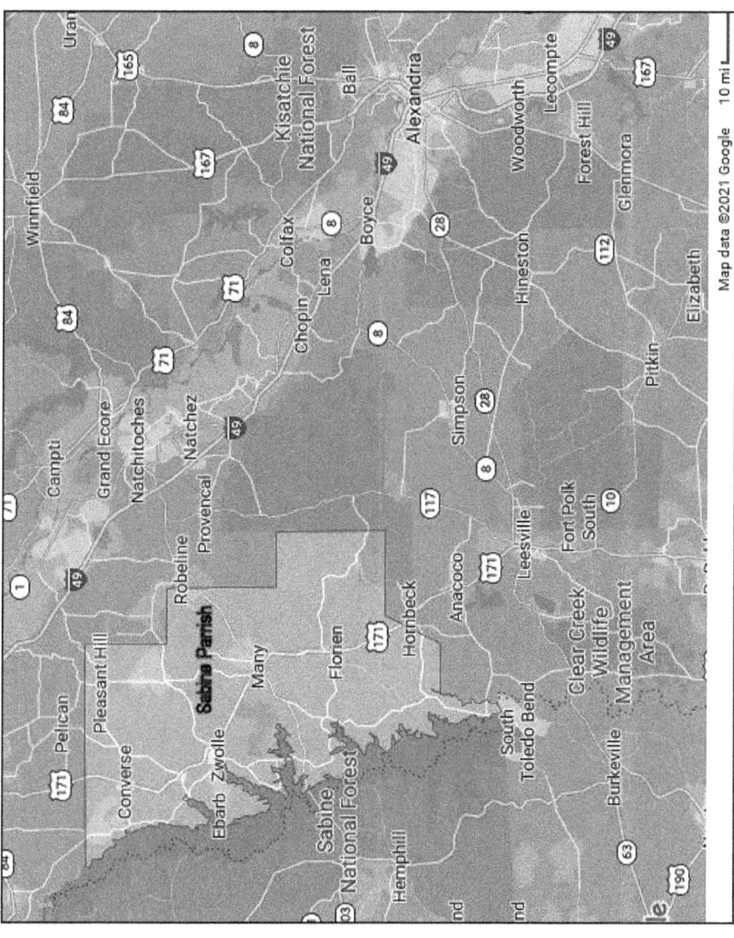

Fig. 6. Map of Sabine Parrish, LA
Google map data © 2015

2

Sawmills

Like so many others looking for work, Montana was attracted to the opportunities in the Louisiana sawmills. Before 1880, timber production in Louisiana was reasonably small and only met local needs. Mills and logging were confined mainly to areas along waterways. By contrast, the so-called "second phase" of lumbering, the "industrial phase," was huge in its output. *"These were the days of giant trees, giant mills and giant lumbermen."*[3]

The lumber boom's impact on Louisiana was enormous. This industry, fueled mainly by out-of-state money, fundamentally changed the look of the state. With a policy of *"cut out and get out,"* priceless natural resources were lost by the millions of acres. In a relatively short time, large sections of the state became vast "stumpscapes" of barren, overly harvested land as mill owners moved on to yet another stand of virgin timber elsewhere in the country.

The early to mid-1920s are generally the end date for the great lumber boom. Almost all of the big Louisiana mills had run out of timber and closed down by this time. As George Alvin Stokes aptly concludes in his 1954 dissertation (Lumbering in Southwest Louisiana,) "The rapidity with which big-time lumbering had entered Louisiana was matched by the speed of its departure."[4]

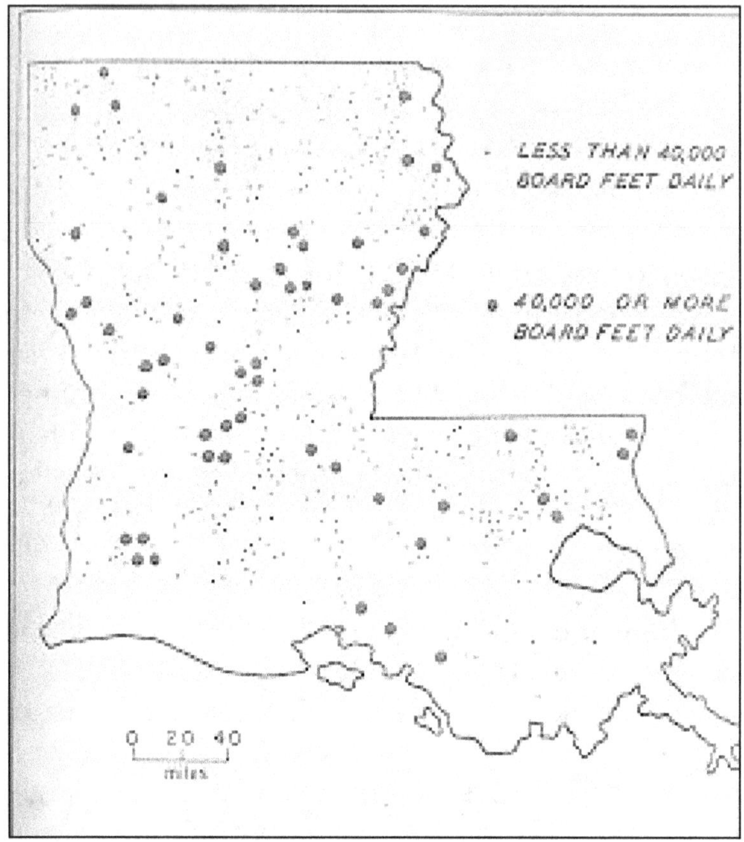

Fig. 7. Lumbering in Southwest La., c. 1937
A Dissertation, Louisiana State University

During this lumber boom, young Montana chased work across Louisiana. He first moved to Barham to work in one of the many sawmills dotted the landscape.

Fig. 8. Logs hauled by Fisher Sawmill commissary.
Sabine Parish Library

Montana worked in at least three sawmills in Louisiana before moving to Texas. One of those sawmills was located in Fisher. The village of Fisher, the last of the old sawmill towns built during the golden age of lumbering in Western Louisiana, was founded by Captain John Barber White and Oliver Williams Fisher. They wanted to locate their sawmill in Montana's hometown of Many. They were rejected because they did not want the noise and dirt accompanying such a business operation. The people were hostile to northerners, hostile to corporations and distinctly unfriendly to anything that might disturb their way of life.[5]

As an alternative, White and Fisher purchased about 10,000 acres in Sabine Parrish, just south of Many, Louisiana. On July 15, 1899, the company was incorporated as Louisiana Long Leaf Lumber Company, better known as the "4-L." Mill operators employed mostly black male workers like Montana to cut and trim the timber, then transport it by river or rail to the sawmills. The logs were sawed into planks and dried. The work was difficult, dangerous and poorly compensated. The 50 to 75 cents per day that most sawmill workers earned in 1910 were the lowest wages paid by a nonagricultural southern industry in the U.S.[6]

Fig. 9. African American floating logs at sawmill.
Library of Congress, Washington, D.C.

Payment in scrip and employer-operated stores were typical throughout the lumber camps. Timber workers complained about the irregularity of their paydays and the numerous deductions employers made for dubious "benefits." The "scrip system" angered mill hands. Companies usually paid their workers with the fake money redeemable only at the company store, where merchants charged exorbitant prices and discounted pay-checks from 15 to 30 percent.

"Teach him how to beat the hired hands out of his half, take the other half and leave them satisfied," one lumber company manager told the math tutor he hired for his young son.[7]

Many plantation owners and lumber companies used such methods to hold their workers in virtual bondage, assisted by an 1892 law that made it illegal for workers to leave employers without paying their debts.

Fig. 10. LA. Lumber Boom, c.1880- 1925.
National Archives and Records Great Lakes Region
Log Loader

Fig. 11. Typical sawmill worker houses in Bogalusa, La.
National Archives and Records Great Lakes Region
The 4-L Company logged out about 150,000 acres before the virgin timber was exhausted in the middle 1930s.

Fig. 12. Great Southern Lumber Mill in Bogalusa, La.
New York Public Library, Zenn Project
Floating Logs to Sawmill

3
Welcome to Lufkin

When Montana and his growing family departed Louisiana, he first took a train to Los Angeles in search of higher wages. However, Montana soon returned with his family to Lufkin. However, he ultimately moved back from Los Angeles, seeking 75 cents an hour in wages.

When Montana and Emma moved to Lufkin in 1919, they found the town of Lufkin in its infancy - controlled and virtually owned by a few extremely powerful, wealthy industrialists.[8]

Fig. 13. African American Mosaic
Library of Congress, Pittsburgh, Pa.
Great Negro Migration from the Farms c. 1930

The town of Lufkin was founded in 1882 at the junction of the H.E. & W.T. and the K.G. & G.S.L. Railroads. It was founded as a railroad stop for the line from Houston, Texas, to Shreveport, Louisiana and is believed to be named for Captain Abraham P. Lufkin. He was a Galveston cotton merchant and city councilman who was a close friend of H.E. &W.T. President Paul Bremond.

"One may justly anticipate the most prosperous future for a railroad center, surrounded by so many valuable and varied natural advantages. That center is Lufkin, located on the dividing ridge between the Neches and Angelina rivers, which facilitates the drainage, either way, of the entire surrounding county, thereby freeing the same of all causes for malaria and noxious exhalations." [9]

Fig. 14. H.E.& W. Texas RR Depot in Lufkin, c. 1907.
Luftex.com
Destroyed by a dynamite explosion in 1913.

In 1885 the entire town tract of 350 acres was laid out in individual lots. Over $10,000 worth of lots were sold to the public. This sale left 90% of the town jointly owned by the railroads. In a few short years, Lufkin had a population of 529 white citizens. The town grew because of its proximity to the railroad and the extensive lumber industry in the surrounding area, similar to what happened in Louisiana. Between 1890 and 1920, a timber boom produced hundreds of sawmills in the Piney Woods.[10]

One of the earliest businesses located about 600 yards southeast of Cotton Square was the steam gin and grist mill of Mr. W.C. Denman. It was an excellent convenience for farmers near town to transact business so close to town. Consequently, he enjoyed local customer support in the area.[11]

Before the town of Lufkin, the place was little more than a settlement, a clearing called Denman Springs. History or lore says, initially, Paul Bremond's Houston, East and West Texas Railroad survey crew was planning a route through then the county seat of Homer. The men became rowdy in a saloon one fateful night and Constable W.B. (Buck) Green put them in jail.

 The arrest so angered the survey crew chief; he allegedly decided to find a route for the railroad that would bypass Homer and pass through Denman Springs. Perhaps the story is more myth than truth. A Railroad 1879 prospectus already indicated that the line would avoid Homer and go through the future site of Lufkin.[12]

Before its incorporation, Lufkin had sought to move the county courthouse, still located at Homer, to their settlement. The first county seat in Angelina was Marion, followed by Jonesville in 1854, only to still move again to Homer in 1858. Due to an election in 1885, it stayed at Homer. However, in November 1891, a "mysterious" fire destroyed Homer's courthouse. One day later, the county commissioners received a petition from Lufkin citizens asking for a new election. When the election was held on January 2, 1892, not surprisingly, Lufkin was chosen as the new county seat.[13]

Much of the economic prosperity of early Lufkin was attributed to three entrepreneurial families: the Kurths, Hendersons and Wieners. At the height of their activity, these three families owned nearly a dozen Texas sawmills, a paper mill, foundries, hotels, movie theaters, railroads, investment companies, newspapers, banks, hospitals and many other businesses. [14]

"After the railroads arrived, the foundation was laid for a way of life and an economy in Angelina County built upon timber and forest products." [15] The history of Lufkin and the surrounding county had not been based on the slave economy like so many other southern communities. It was and mainly remained agrarian throughout the period before the Civil War. In fact, in 1861, it was one of only a few Texas counties that voted to reject secession.[16]

Unfortunately, around 1880, much as Louisiana had squandered its rich timber resources with inefficient and wasteful harvesting practices, Angelina and Lufkin fell into the same dire situation. Luckily, this industry understood that it must embrace conservation and sustainable maintenance to enjoy long-term viability. This foresight allowed the lumber industry to remain a force in the area well into the 1950s and beyond.[17]

If Montana thought life in Lufkin would be much easier than Louisiana because of its growing economic prosperity, he was sadly mistaken. A sawmill operator in East Texas, W.T. Carter, reportedly refused to purchase an automatic device to flip and turn logs on the saw carriage because the invention "couldn't trade at the commissary." He was referring to the lucrative profits some unscrupulous owners of the commissaries enjoyed.

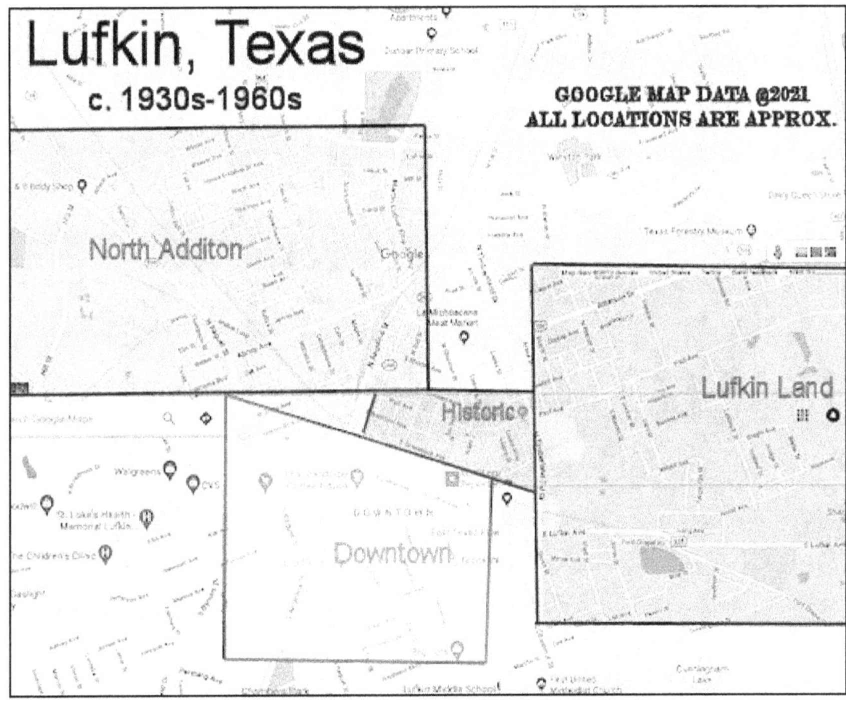

Fig. 15. City of Lufkin, c. 1930 - 1960s
Google (2021) map data
Original Map using approximate site locations referenced by contemporary inhabitants

Fig. 16. First Street, c. 1940.

City of Lufkin.com

Fig. 17. First Street, c. 2006.

(Author's personal photograph)

Fig. 18. Angelina Four, c. 1940.
Library of Congress, Washington, D.C.
Kelty's Lumber Company

The World's Fair of 1893 helped drive the popularity of
southern pine as a building material. The Angelina County
Lumber Company, founded by Joseph Kurth, Sr. and others
in 1887 in the small community of Keltys (just outside
Lufkin), immensely enjoyed the growth of this product.[18]

Growth fueled the birth of many changes. No longer was Lufkin just a destination for farmers to set or distribute their products. It was becoming an actual business community.

In 1924, members of the Lufkin Ladies Auxiliary of the Chamber of Commerce purchased a lot on Ellis Avenue across from the Lufkin High School. They moved the library into a former kindergarten.[19]

Farmers who worked the land for generations found their agrarian society supplemented with the beginnings of the industrial age. Farmers, sharecroppers and all who serve them faced an efficient and mechanized competition.

Fig. 19. Negro Sharecropper
"Hoe Culture in the South. Library of Congress, Washington D.C.
Leaving the fields for the sawmills and foundries

4

The Architect

Will Ingram (Rev. Bettie Kennedy's adopted father.) built many of the houses and sites for black businesses in the area during this time. He built large residential/ commercial sections of town, including Joe's Quarters, Walkers Quarters, Nesbitt Quarters, Jake Stroud Quarters and many other Negro neighborhood developments in Lufkin. He also built many churches, including Goodwill Baptist Church, Long Chapel Church, First United Methodist Church and First Baptist Church.

Ingram reportedly built 125 houses in Lufkin. Sam Hyman and Ben Taylor were the financiers of many of these projects. He built houses for Hyman and the Largent House. For Dr. P.A. Simond, he built his home, six rental dwellings and a clinic. The clinic is still standing, called Packard's clinic.[20]

Ingram worked for a white man, Joe Stefano, who built Joe's Quarters. To support his active construction business, Will Ingram hired six local black men: They were - Smitty Cole, Henry Cole, Marvin Jackson, Robert Jackson, Montana Lillie (the author's grandfather) and U.S. Smith. They were all from Cedar Grove. Two of the men were left-handed by design. He put left-handed people on one side and right-handed people on the other. Ingram felt that he could build houses faster that way. As a tribute to his legacy, these men continued to pursue carpentry careers after his death.

Many believed that Will Engram was a master of mathematics, geometry and algebra despite a 3rd-grade education. Earnest McGowan, retired, former Houston city councilman, said, *"Will figured out the materials he needed for the houses. He did the electricity, the plumbing and everything else. He was excellent in figuring the dimensions down to six and seven grains of sawdust."*[21]

It was probably an accurate statement to categorize Will Ingram as one of the first blacks to join the middle class in Lufkin. He was believed to be the first black to own a car, the first phone (number 794) and owned the first indoor toilet. He was well dressed in striped overalls that were well-ironed and starched. He had a bank account to draw down for cash as needed for his jobs. He purchased materials from Angelina Lumber, Taylor Hardware, Abney and Medford and Sam Hyman. This business activity occurred from 1928 to 1935.[22]

Ingram would build the entire house, including plumbing and electrical. Then he would turn over the key to the new, proud owner when finished. Ingram made the cabinets for the houses he built. As his illness progressed and the end of his illustrious life was approaching, he hired Montana Lillie and U.S. Smith to complete the three homes that Ingram was building before his death. He told them how to complete it from his bedside.[23]

Fig. 20. Angelina Hardwood Lumber Co., c. 1930s.
Luftex.com
Office and Commissary

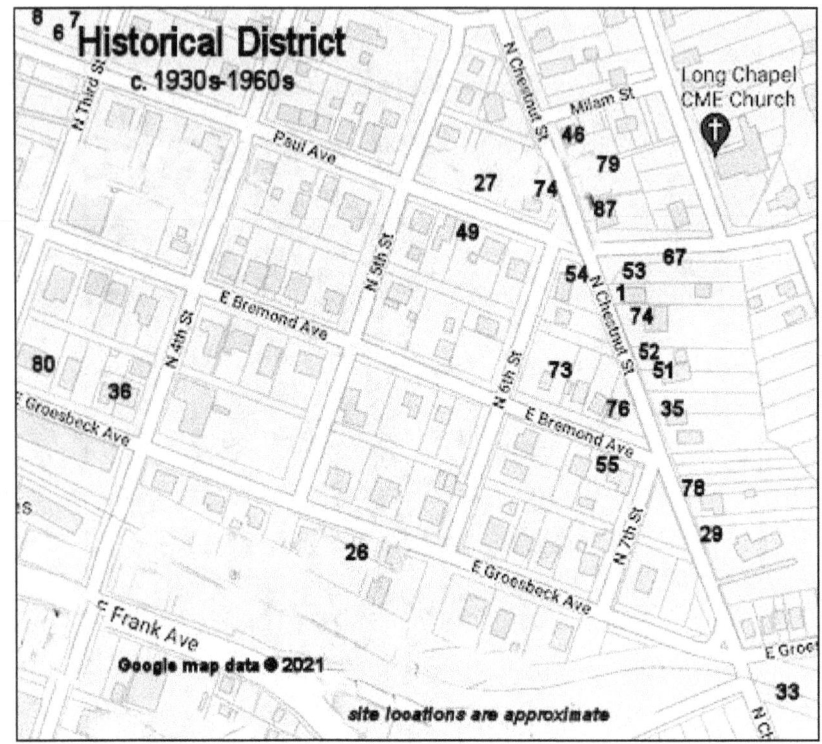

Fig. 21. Black Historic District, c. 1930s – c. 1950s.
Google (2021) map data
Original Map using approximate site locations referenced by contemporary inhabitants

Lufkin, Texas
Black Historic District

	SITE	LOCATION
1	Lucky Ward School	431 North Chestnut
26	Historic District	Groesbeck, Bremond, Chestnut, Paul
27	Joe Stefano's Joe's Quarters	Chestnut & Lining, where Inez Tims apartments are now
29	Sadie Hackney's grocery store	408 Chestnut
36	Hotel Alamo	121 Groesbeck
46	Joe's Movie show	Lightning St, Joes Quarters
49	L.C. Lillie Blue Room	N. Chestnut St.
50	First Black Grocery Store (Carl Hackney)	408 or 418 N. Chestnut St.
51	Shack Town	Lining St. behind Chestnut
52	Masonic Lodge Lodge	Above Dr. Simmons' office on 422 Chestnut
53	First Long Chapel CME	Groesbeck &410 N. Chestnut St.
54	New Long Chapel CME	514 Lining St and Paul
55	Goodwill Baptist	Lufkin Ave & 909 Clark
67	George Washington Carver School	Timberland Drive
73	Will Ingram's (Bettie Kennedy) home	402 Chestnut St.
74	Dr. Simmons' office	422 Chestnut (first floor)
76	December Taxi Stand	338 Chestnut St.
78	Evie Ingram beauty Shop	408 Chestnut St.
79	Will Ingram Grocery store	408 Chestnut St.
80	Brookshire Brothers home	Corner of Groesbeck & 4th
87	Hattie Mannos Restaurant	718 Paul Ave
88	Gipson Funeral Home	S. Chestnut St.

Table 1. Sites for Black Historic District

Original Map using approximate site locations referenced by contemporary inhabitants (see fig. 20)

Chestnut Street was part of the Negro Historical area of Lufkin. There was a heavy concentration of blacks living from Groesbeck Street to Paul Avenue. Across from Bremond and Chestnut, whites in the area lived there. From 7th Street and Chestnut were primary white residences. Groesbeck was where the Jewish families lived. On Groesbeck, there was a concentration of Dutch people across the track. The Negro Historic District bounded by Bremond, Chestnut and Paul represented the foundation of the Negro presence during the early days of this East Texas community.

Groesbeck and 4th street corner is where the Brookshire's lived - Oscar, Eugene, R.A. and Lois Ann. Their first store was downtown, where the county jail is now, in 1916 or 1917.

Fig. 22. Brookshire Brothers, c. 1921.
Countyline Magazine.com

Jewish families, white families and black families all lived in the area. In later years, Jewish families such as - The Abrams had the Abrams Store downtown, which later became the Cannon and Parker store were in this area.

Fig. 23. Harry Abram, c. 1960.
Texas Jewish Historical Society

Abram lived on Paul Street just outside of the district. Chestnut was the center of the neighborhood and the early beginnings of a thriving community. At 408, Mr. Sadie Hackney worked as a clerk in the grocery store. He later owned his own store. At 402 Chestnut, Will Ingram built a home for his wife, Evie. He designed it so she could live comfortably and work from home. He built her a washroom and the washroom had a wash pot right outside the door. Inside the washroom area, there was a ringer-type washing machine with three tubs. The first tub was for clear water, the second tub was for bluing (a product used to improve the appearance of clothes, particularly whites), and the last was the ringing of the clothes. There was a drying area with a heater in case of rain or cold. Will Ingram eventually built another home on Chestnut Street. This location became a grocery store, a beauty shop, and two apartments.

The Negro community was growing, so no existing asset was wasted or torn down. It was simply repurposed for someone or something else. It's why schools became homes and rent houses became barbershops. During the Depression, Evie had a garden for fresh vegetables and a hen house for eggs and chicken. In the garden, she grew beans, okra and cantaloupes.[24]

5
Daily Routine

Lunch often consisted of boiled peas and greens. Frequently, in the morning, there were freshly made flapjacks (little pancakes). During the week, 'corncakes' were served with syrup. On Sundays, there was flour cake, boiled food, cornbread, and stew meat. Chicken was served in a variety of ways – baked, fried, stewed, broiled, with dumplings and with cornbread dressing.[25]

Walker Quarters was almost directly behind the Congo Club, which stood behind two railroad tracks. Most homes had three rooms: the living room, bedroom, and living room. The bedroom was reserved for the parents to sleep. The kitchen was for cooking and the eating place since there was no special provision made for dining. Meals were cooked, served and eaten there. The third room was meant for everything else. It had to accommodate all the children at night regardless of family size. Otherwise, they would be forced to sleep on makeshift beds someplace else. Essential city utilities like water, gas and sewage were not available for individual homes in the black neighborhoods. At best, they had to be shared with nearby houses. There was virtually no inside plumbing, no bathrooms and no running water. There was usually an outside toilet which was just a pit dug into the ground with a little shell built around it where a person could take care of their bodily needs.[26]

The crude toilet would usually serve three or four households. There was no individual toilet. The same thing was true of water service. A single water faucet was provided in the yard and that one water faucet would also serve those same three or four households.

Fig. 24. "Shotgun" houses on Chestnut St., c. 1950.
(Author's family photograph)

Residents would gather water outside and bring it inside to wash clothes, clean dishes and bath. There were no individual gas lines either. So heating was provided by wooden, kerosene or coal oil heaters.[27]

Fig. 25. Third Ward Houston shotgun houses, c. 1970.
Wikipedia Commons

A common theme throughout this story is the fact that local blacks would find a way to grow, raise and cook their food. They grew their vegetables. Some had fruit trees. Many raised hogs, cows, chickens and most households frequently hunted and fished for supplemental meat. With these animals, they were able to harvest eggs and milk. Many women knew the long-forgotten skill of churning butter. Water from the common line provided by the city was supplemented with deep wells in more remote areas.

"Well, you had to accept what they had to offer, you know, you couldn't do anything about it. That is the way we used to do around here."[28] Carrington

Fig. 27. Life for the poor Is difficult.
"One of Tenant Families on Their Porch," Library of
Congress, Washington. D.C.

During WWII, authorities would have children go through the woods looking for scrap metal and bones of carcasses of dead animals. Sometimes they would dismiss school on occasions to perform this war effort. They would take the bones to make soap or other goods from them. Of course, the scrap metal was melted down and made into tools and military weapons.[29]

Jones Park was originally for whites only. The city later gave that park to the blacks. There was swimming in the lake and a dance floor. When blacks began to occupy more and more territory in North Lufkin around Jones Lake, black folk began requesting more access to these public facilities. Then after the 1954 (Board vs. Education Supreme Court decision), their voices grew louder.

At this time, things began to tear down desegregation. [30] (Note: The decision effectively overturned Plessy v. Ferguson.) This decision paved the way for integration and was considered a landmark civil rights victory.[31] Many blacks at the time thought that city leaders were growing concerned about the increasing interest in Negroes using Winston Park (near North Addition). Blacks felt that Lufkin leadership had decided to improve Jones Lake Park and make it a Negro facility to allow Winston Park to stay all white. The same could be valid for the construction of the new Dunbar School. The need for a new school had existed for years. The original Dunbar on Leach Street was inadequate. It was felt that it took the Supreme Court Decision to spur change. Some thought that the leaders decided to put the school in a location in the North Addition so that the new construction would be less objectionable to the white population.[32]

The social life in Lufkin for young people and teenagers was mainly three things - socials, the park and dance clubs. Usually, there were 'socials' during school was every Friday night. Socials were local dances for the teens that started around 8 o'clock and ended around eleven o'clock. At that time, couples had to split up and go to their respective homes *"you had a little social where you danced and tried to find you a favorite girl to walk home."* **Rhodes**.

At the time, at Jones Lake Park, they built a platform out on the back. It didn't have a swimming pool, but it had a platform out on the bank with a jukebox on Friday nights and Saturday nights.[33]

"The most exclusive part of town was probably the Montrose area going toward Memorial Hospital. Abney was pretty much the dividing line, Abney back north on up Kelty's and all up the tracks

were where blacks lived. If you were found anywhere else from the south side of Abney back toward Memorial Hospital, all back in that area was exclusively white and you did not find yourself in that area after sundown. "[34] **Rhodes**

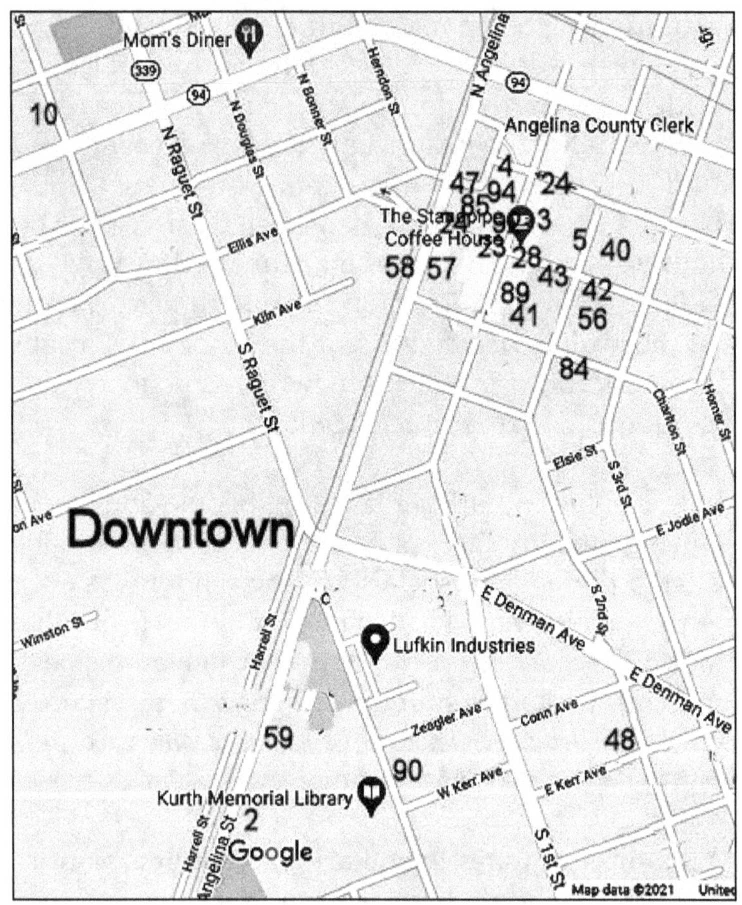

Fig. 26. Lufkin, Texas - Downtown c. 1930s - 1950s.
Google (2021) map data
Original Map using approximate site locations referenced by contemporary inhabitants

2	Lufkin Foundry & Machine	S. Angelina St & Kerr (one blk from H.E.& W.T. depot)
4	Ruby's Cafe	Frank St, just as you come out of the underpass to your left
5	Charlie Gann Restaurant	Facing library
7	Lufkin Cotton Gin, Wrecking yard/salvage	S. 3rd St, 1 blk S. of Burke Ave. Abney, across from Uncle Felix
8	Daniel Hotel	next to cotton gin, Abney
23	Former train station, then fire station	Douglass & Franklin, by the track
24	Lufkin High School	S. Raquet, SE Corner Ellis Ave
28	Lynn Theatre	Downtown Frank, 1st St
40	Finis Price, blacksmith	Downtown near City Hall, 3rd Street, 1930s), 212 Burke
41	1000 Alley Entertainment Center	Downtown 1st St & Angelina, where Lufkin Conroe Tele is now
42	Big Barber's barbershop	1000 Alley
43	Maggie McCoy beauty shop	1000 Alley
47	Buzzard Roost (Lynn Theatre)	Upper floor of Lynne Theatre
48	Texan Theatre	1st St across from Lynn Theatre
56	Pool Hall, domino shack	1000 Alley
57	Fire station	Where Kurth Library is (Douglass & Franklin), West Side Cotton Sq
58	Train station	Near where Kurth Library is, Douglass & Frankline besides the tracks on Angelina, Cotton Square, West side
59	Cotton Square	built later, where train station was. One blk west of First at the intersection of Lufkin Ave.
62	Angelina Hotel and Coffee Shop	Corner of S. First & Shepard, On Abney, Walker Quarters

84	Abney Hardware	Downtown became Cannon & Parker's
85	Harry Abram & Sons Dry Goods	112 Cotton Square, 112 S. First
89	Pine Theatre	Current location on Main st.
90	Kurth Library (current location)	709 South Raquet St., W. Kerr Ave
91	Kurth Memorial Library (original location)	Where the fire station used to be, near the train station on Douglas & Franklin besides the tracks on Angelina St.
92	Perry Brothers	104 Cotton Square

Table 2. Site locations Lufkin Downtown

Original Map using approximate site locations referenced by contemporary inhabitants (see fig. 25)

In the early 1920s, Lufkin had a curfew that required everyone to be off the streets at nine o'clock. An electric whistle where the former fire station was (the same site as the former train station in downtown Lufkin on Douglas and Franklin) would blow every night at nine o'clock. Unless you were a policeman or had official business, you were required to be off the streets. It's unclear whether this curfew only applied to blacks or all Lufkinites.[35]

Fig. 27. Fire Station and City Hall, c. 1902.

Luftex.com

The standpipe is seen behind the building.

Although all homeowners paid taxes for municipal services, local black residents recall the frustration of seeing their streets not being paved. They recall an example where the city was paving North Raquet Street. After they passed Abney Street, there was a black church called the New Zion Church. The city paved the road until they got to the ice house and stopped just outside the black neighborhood. The same held true on Paul Avenue, where the paving stopped once it reached the black community.[36]

Fig. 28. Black men working on the rail.
Iowaculture.gov

In the 1940s, many people came to Lufkin because of the growing war economy. Jobs were plentiful when the foundries began to make guns and war equipment and tanks.

Negroes felt that they should maintain a low profile and stay in their neighborhoods. Many thought that there could be problems if they tried to socialize with whites. Although organizations like the Klu Klux Klan were not particularly active in Lufkin, there remained a sense of caution as it involved interracial mingling.

Also, there were the infamous Jim Crow laws enacted across the South. Negroes could go to the movies and shop downtown. However, they had to use the back door of some stores and were just not allowed inside others.

Fig. 29. Jim Crow mandated segregation.
History.com

Jim Crow Laws existed in Lufkin also. Many white stores, such as J.C. Penny's, Perry Brothers and Woolworths, allowed blacks to use the back door freely. For other establishments, no blacks were allowed inside. For other white businesses, blacks had to stand off to the side to be served.[37]

Fig. 30. Downtown, c. 1950.
Luftex.com
Perry Brothers on First Street next to Rexall

There were incidents when Negroes occasionally refused to follow the rules. Once, a light-skinned Negro was arrested sitting in the white section of Pines Theatre. Another time, a Negro got into a fight with a white man. Confident that there would be reprisals, he quietly left Lufkin, moved to Kansas and never returned.[38]

Despite the institutional and societal challenges faced by the African-American community, they continued to charge forth in their efforts to forge a better life for their families and themselves.

Montana and millions of other men probably didn't realize it, but they helped America transform from an agrarian economy to the Industrial Age.

He was part of an Age that would propel this nation into prominence on the world stage. He managed to secure a job at Lufkin Foundry as a laborer for 30 cents/hour. Lufkin Foundry was, in fact, in its infancy, having just opened for business less than 20 years earlier. Little did each appreciate that Lufkin Foundry would provide a place of employment for Montana and his bloodline for over a century.

In the 1920s and 30s, Lufkin enjoyed the fruits of the industrial age, which meant good wages at the Lufkin and Texas Foundry, even for unskilled or semi-skilled Negros. Jobs were plentiful. From the wages grew a sort of Negro business class.

There were also jobs available on the numerous railroads that dotted the South. Unfortunately, it seemed that most of the positions open to Negroes were service-oriented such as porters.

Fig. 31. Pullman porter on the train.
National Museum of American History

Fig. 32 Negro Brakeman
Washington Book Publishers

Blacks wanted access to the higher-paying and more prestigious brakeman positions. One of the higher-paying semi-skilled jobs available to a few African Americans was the brakeman position.

Negros only got the opportunity to be brakeman after a spirited petition presented to the Southern Pacific President around 1920. The brakemen working for the railroad had a booster club whose members were their wives. The relative affluence was evident when this club hosted an entertainment and fashion show at the Cotton Club. Brakemen were Lufkin's first Negro middle class. They enjoyed a better standard of living. They had nice cars and dressed very nicely and lived in nice homes in the Negro community. There was great respect and prestige for wives who were married to brakemen.

During these early years, Montana's family rented a house from New Zion Baptist Church for $5/month (Adams Street in 1935-1940). About this time, they welcomed into the world their first child Berta Mae born in October 1920. Whether seeking a larger home or for some other reason, the young family moved to another rented house owned by the black First Baptist Church in Lufkin. The fact that these rent homes were almost in eyesight of his eventual homestead on Chestnut Street could have been coincidental or the culmination of a dream he had that would take another 15 years of hard work to realize. Montana continued to find work at increasingly higher wages. By 1940, he was a Crane Operator, making $700 a year (at the Federal Poverty Line of $13,000 in today's dollars.)

He ultimately decided that jobs as unskilled or semi-skilled laborers were insufficient for him financially and spiritually. At that point, Montana decided to become a carpenter. Those skills or at least that desire was, certainly challenged when he bought the 428/430 (one building, two front doors and two addresses) Chestnut property in 1936. At that point, the property had been many things but not a home. He began to make the modifications that would endure for decades through storms, tornadoes and hurricanes.

Later, Montana expanded the 428 Chestnut house to allow Vera's (his daughter, my mother) burgeoning family room to grow. Her two youngest sons shared a bed and bedroom with Vera and her husband Clark, while their two oldest children shared another bedroom. Montana knocked down walls and essentially doubled their side of the homestead incorporating rooms that previously served as Lucky Ward School classrooms and barbershops.

Apparently, his skills or desire must have caught the attention of Will Ingram (The Architect). Ingram hired him to help build, among other structures, the more significant part of the original Goodwill Baptist Church and also the New Zion Baptist Church. Before the prevalence of electricity in the Negro neighborhood, church fires were not entirely uncommon. A combination of wood, numerous lanterns and irregular occupation were just the ingredients that fed the rebuild industry. Not to embellish the significance of these two feats, the story told and retold over the years claims that Montana built both churches by himself from the ground level. Perhaps that was an exaggeration. However, Montana could read and prepare blueprints that rivaled educated architects despite his limited education.

Fig. 33. Dr. Percy Simond, c. 1955.

Montana also helped build or remodel several homes, such as those owned by Dr. Percy Simond and Davis properties. When it was all said and done, Montana helped build churches that stand today, decades later.

6
Lufkin Land

Lufkin Land was located within the corporate city limits of Lufkin. The community was surrounded by a sawmill owned by Lufkin Land and Lumber Company (4-L). At its peak in the early 1900s, The 4-L had a commissary for its employees, a drug store, a meat market, several other stores, a company office, a company doctor and its own grammar school (although the Lufkin school system technically managed it).

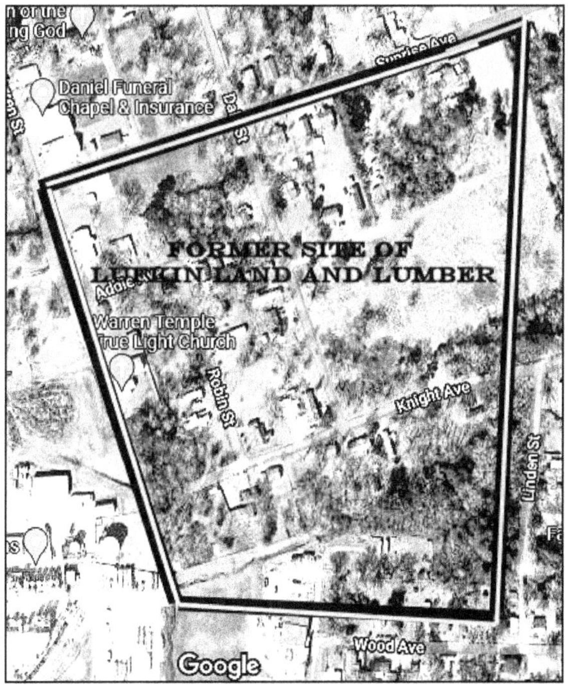

Fig. 34, Site of former Lufkin Land & Lumber Company.
@2022 Google Maps

The town's population reached about 300 people at its peak — the community located along Lufkin Avenue west of what is now Timberland Drive. *"A mixed-race crew was employed at both the mill and the camp. At the camp, the Negroes were used in the steel gang, in the loading crew, and some few sawyers (flat-heads) were Negroes. The Negroes were used in the dangerous places."*[39] In the 1900s, a lake near the Veterans of Foreign Wars building was a part of the lumber company's sawmill pond. Houses for the sawmill families were built throughout the community. The finest homes were occupied by mill managers standing along Lufkin Avenue.

Fig. 35. Typical East Texas Sawmill, c. 1910.
Center for American History

The Lufkin Land and Lumber Company was established around 1900 by several lumbermen with other sawmilling interests in Angelina and other counties. It was the first and only large sawmill to be located within the city limits of Lufkin or any other established town.[40]

Lufkin Land was almost in another world. Within the area, there was a black part and a white part. Given the limited transportation, some families who owned a car and lived in North Lufkin didn't go to Lufkin Land.

Lufkin had an abundance of sawmills processing the plentiful pine trees in the Pineywoods. The Lone Star Sawmill was in Lufkin Land. The pond is still there. Also, about four mill houses are still standing on Wood Street and an adjacent street there.[41] You can still see the pond that floated the logs near Wood Street and Sunrise. The Vaughns' owned a creosote plant near there also. The area immediately around the businesses was considered the white area, Negroes lived farther away. The commissary was nearby on Denman Avenue. Its location and purpose were typical of the sawmill plants of the era.

Many Negroes at that time considered Lufkin Land the heart of Lufkin. Many Negroes in the New Addition relocated to the area, searching for better-paying jobs. Also, there was another sawmill at the former Walmart (now Sam's) site.[42]

Fig. 36. Ties awaiting creosote treatment.
Wikipedia Commons

In 1905, the 4-L was sold to Long Bell Lumber Company and operated for 25 years. [43]   It did not survive the Great Depression.

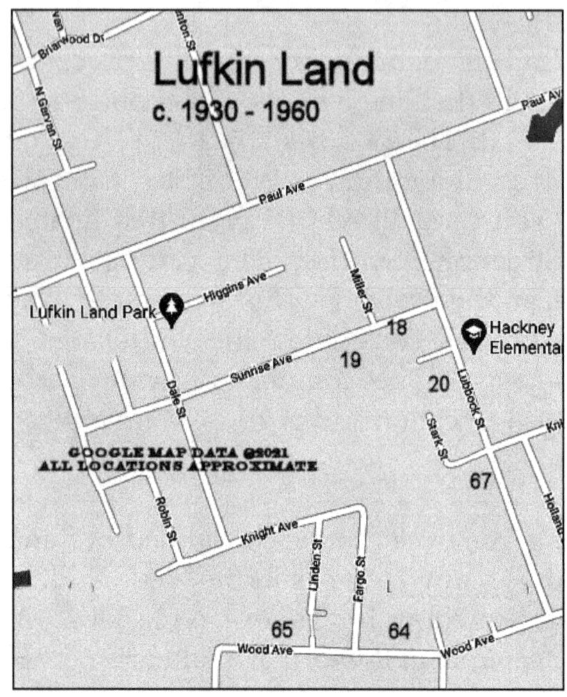

Fig. 37. Lufkin, Texas - Lufkin Land, c. 1930s-1960s

Google (2021) map data

Original Map using approximate site locations referenced by contemporary inhabitants

18	McClendon's House of Blue Lights	near Lufkin Land
19	McClendon's Paradise Inn	Lufkin Land
20	Lone Star Sawmill	Lufkin Land near Sam's now
33	Long Bell Lumber Co	Clark and East end Calvert
64	Sawmill	Lufkin Land, Wood & Sunrise at the pond
65	Creosote Plant	Denman Ave.
86	Carver Elementary (original)	Behind Albertson - 111N Timberland dr, Served Lufkin Land children too.

Table 3. Site locations for Lufkin Land.

7

Nazi Camps in Lufkin

Prisoners of war (POWs) began arriving in America in early 1943 with the first shipment of 150,000 men. After that, some 20,000 to 60,000 prisoners a month were housed for the duration of WWII. According to the **Handbook of Texas Online**, *"When the war was over, there were 425,000 enemy prisoners in 511 main and branch camps throughout the United States."*[44]

The people of Lufkin were not initially told that Nazi POWs would be confined in their community. After the news was released, some folks visited the camp to see themselves. As time progressed, the ever-increasing arrival of additional prisoners only sparked local interest. The prisoners were strategically sent to Lufkin to help provide labor to support one of East Texas's principal industries - sawmill operations.[45]

Southland Paper Mills, Inc. began production of newsprint in 1940. However, when America entered the war, mill production began to slip due to a lack of labor to deliver wood to the mill. This growing manpower shortage caused Southland Mill leadership to decide that Nazi labor could be used to offset the lack of American manpower. Soon after that, wartime officials agreed. Texas had twice as many POW camps like any other state because of space and climate, according to the **Handbook**. The 12 Texas POW camps that opened in August 1943 had nearly tripled in a year. "

The Geneva Conventions of 1929 requires that prisoners of war be moved to a climate similar to that where they are captured; apparently, it was thought that the climate of Texas is similar to that of North Africa," the **Handbook** state.

These POW camps were built like military barracks. They had rows of cots and footlockers and could house up to 4000 prisoners each. The Nazi barracks had central heat using potbelly stoves. The guard towers were located along with double barbed-wire fencing. The German POWs at the Lufkin camp were paid 80 cents an hour for forced labor to perform logging and support pulpwood operations.[46]

Fig. 38. Former POW Camp in Lufkin.
The Lufkin Daily News, 10 February 2007
*State Historical Marker in WWII Prisoner Camp Site
on S. Racquet St., 2007*

Fig. 39. WWII soldiers with captured Nazi flag, 1945.
Harry S. Truman Library & Museum
In the photograph, one must only wonder how was Sgt. Hugh D. Thompson (2nd from the left) from Lufkin was treated when he returned to Lufkin after this successful campaign?

From Camp Lufkin, the prisoners were delivered to the forests where they harvested pines and hauled them to Lufkin on pulpwood trucks. The work crews usually consisted of twelve prisoners, a driver provided by Southland, and a single guard with a submachine gun or Browning automatic rifle. The prisoners were so productive that other POW camps were established in the vicinity. A second Lufkin camp, which eventually housed 500 prisoners, was opened on Lufkin Middle School's present site. Another camp opened beside the Angelina and Neches River Railroad between Chireno and Etoile in Nacogdoches County.[47]

According to an Associated Press article provided by Jonathan Gerland with **The History Center** in Diboll, in June 1944, the Lufkin prisoners went on a labor strike to protest the camp commander's orders for the Nazis to increase their production beyond the standard output experienced in the industry by American workers.

In an online discussion of prisoner of war treatment, an Angelina County native wrote of the Lufkin POW camp, "*My mother told me they held dances in the camp on Saturday nights and a fair number of local women would go to them. And there was some fooling around. She knew several women whose husbands were overseas but who got pregnant by a POW.*"[48] It seemed odd that the Nazi prisoners whose sworn duty was to kill Americans and if successful, enslave this country were so generously accepted. While at the same time, Negro soldiers in the U.S. military were so often mistreated upon their return from service. A white, two-story house located off North Raguet Street (North of the city) on property owned by the U.S. Forest Service is the last reminder of this camp's existence.[49]

Fig. 40. "Rothammer", Former POW Camp in Lufkin
The Lufkin Daily News, 10 February 2007
German POW Camp Marker
This stone, believed to have been inscribed by a German prisoner of war, still stands off Raquet Street in northwest Lufkin. Photo by Jonathan Gerland, September 2005.[50]

8

Black Wall Street

There is an odd dichotomy in America when it comes to black-owned businesses. It seems like, despite the legal, financial and social barriers throughout history, there was a time when the entrepreneurial spirit in black neighborhoods was much more intense. Oddly, black businesses were aided by the undeniable fact that segregation and Jim Crow Laws limited the choices of the Negro consumer. Their opportunities to secure essential services such as food, groceries, and entertainment were severely limited to some white establishments that often treated the Negro dollars with less respect than the white customers using the same currency. Black consumers could often stay in their neighborhoods and support their friends and neighbors. It wasn't just Lufkin, but all over the United States. Houston's Wards, Harlem, Tulsa Black Wall Street section, et al., were all thriving with black businesses and commerce. It should be noted that many white-owned companies in Lufkin valued the Negro consumer, if not equally, certainly concerning their purchasing power.

The vibrancy of the Negro business was alive and well during those difficult social times. This passage from the Dunbar High School 1964 Yearbook quantifies the status: *"Negro citizens in Lufkin endeavor to make their contribution to community life in business as in professional life and labor. The survey made by the high school civics class in 1955 shows that Negroes in Lufkin operate: four barber shops, seventeen beauty shops, two mortuaries, one blacksmith shop, ten cafes, five construction agencies, one cleaning and pressing shop, eight grocery stores, three garages, three hotels, one radio repair shop, two taxi lines, three service stations, one newsstand, and two washaterias."* [51]

Lufkin had black-owned businesses for sure. They were tucked away in Historical Lufkin, Lufkin Land, Old Addition, New Addition Lufkin and even parts of downtown. Joe Stephano had a different approach. He was a white man who catered to the black consumer. He was an Italian who owned a theatre called Joe's Show in Joe's Quarters for blacks on Lightning Street. Joe's Quarters was located where Inez Tims' Apartments are now. Will Ingram built those houses for Joe.

Joe's Show had white and black-oriented movies, including *Amos and Andy*. Tickets cost a nickel to go to the movies. The theatre was for blacks only. [52]

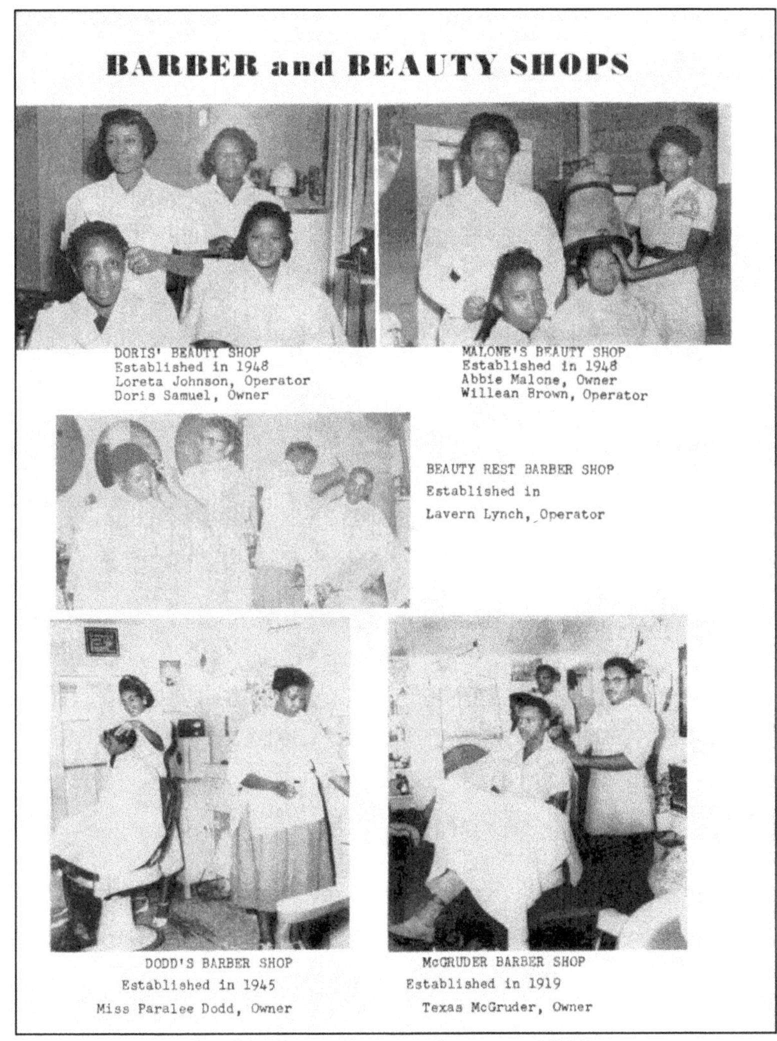

Fig. 41. Negro Beauty Shops, c. 1956.
"The Mirror 1955-56," Negro Chamber of Commerce and Dunbar High School

During those times, the foundation of African Americans was service-based.   There was a seamless understanding of business owner and customer needs, whether it was barber shops, restaurants or beauty shops.

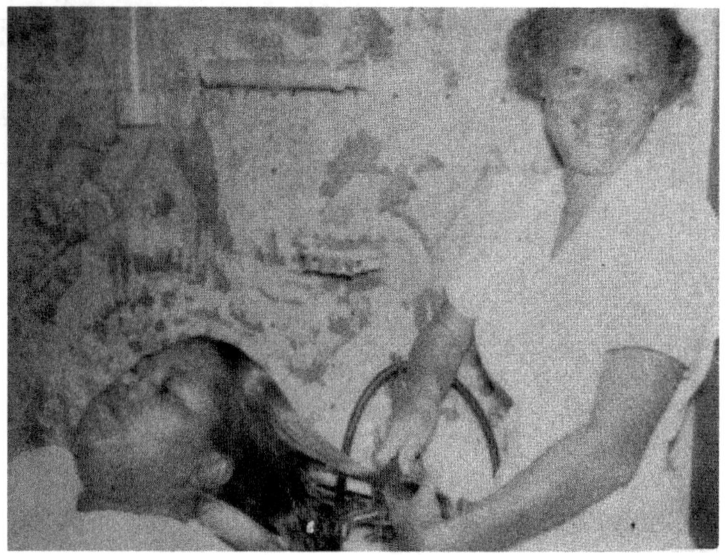

Fig. 42. Smith Beauty Shop, c. 1956.
"The Mirror 1955-56," Negro Chamber of Commerce and Dunbar High School
1950s beauty shop

Robert Tatum owned the only African American cleaners during the 1950s and 60s. Here, the neighborhood entrusted to him their finest Sunday best.

Fig. 43. Houston Tatum Cleaners, c. 1956.
"The Mirror 1955-56," Negro Chamber of Commerce and
Dunbar High School

Fig. 44. Haircutting In Front of General Store, c. 1939.
Wikipedia Commons
From the Past

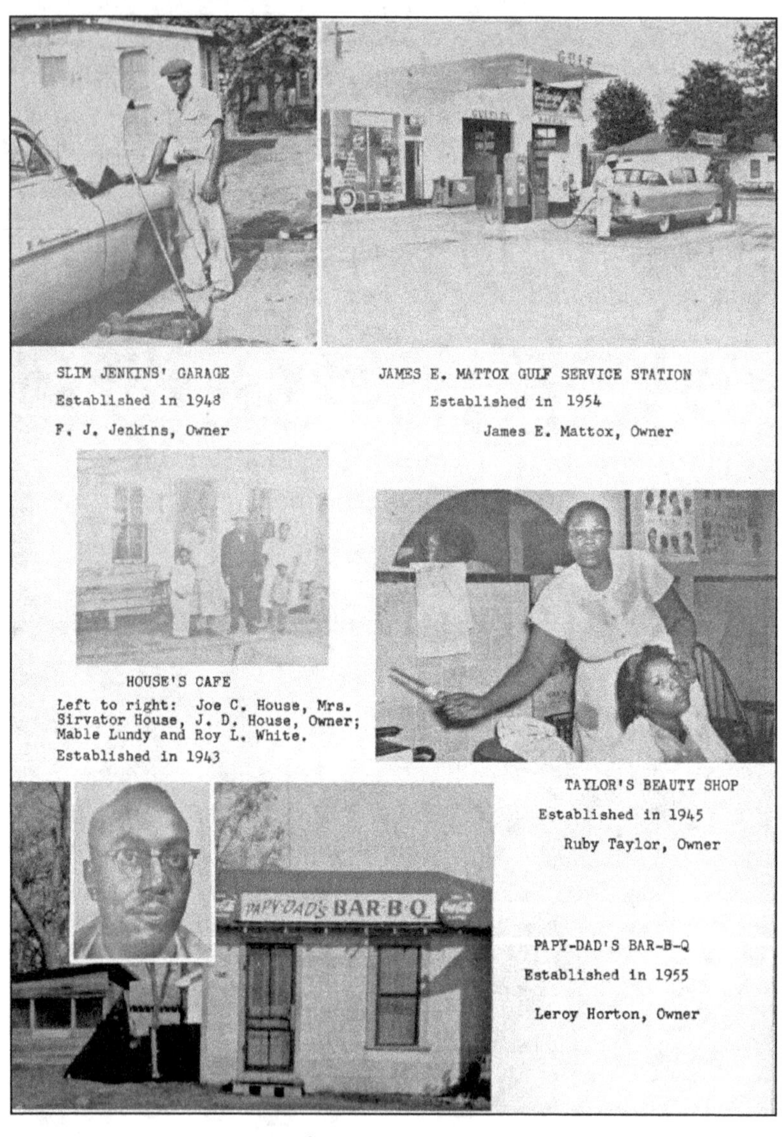

Fig. 45. Local Negro Businesses, c. 1956.

"The Mirror 1955-56," Negro Chamber of Commerce and Dunbar High School

The Lynn Theatre was located downtown on First Street. It was open to blacks and whites, although the two races were kept separate. Negroes were only allowed upstairs in what was called the "Buzzard Roost."[53]

Fig. 46. The Lynne Theatre, c. 1940s.
Cinema Treasures, Cinematreasures. org

The Pines Theatre was one of the cinemas that initially allowed whites only and later opened the upstairs to blacks. Ironically, balcony seating at theatres today is premium priced and considered perhaps the best way to view a movie. The Texan Theatre across from Lynn's Theatre never opened to blacks.[54]

Fig. 47. Pines Theatre in Lufkin, Texas, c. 1940.
Wikipedia Commons

Gipson Funeral home was the first Lufkin business that buried both black and white people. Latimore had a funeral home on Angelina Street. Later, the black-owned Pace's funeral home opened on Leach Street.

Fig. 48. Tims Funeral Home, c. 1956.
"The Mirror 1955-56," Negro Chamber of Commerce and Dunbar High School
(222 Leach Street)
*"Day and Night Ambulance Service
Burial Insurance for the entire family."*

Inez D. Tims owned Tim's Funeral home. He operated in the Masonic building until he built his own building next door on Leach Street. He previously worked for Pace Mortuary.[55]

Fig. 49. Lewis Service Station & Malone Barbershop
The Mirror 1955-1955-56," Negro Chamber of
Commerce and Dunbar High School

The Davis Colonial Mortuary and Burial Association located at 1311 Keltys St. was founded in 1948 by Mr. and Mrs. Ozell H. Davis. It has been under the direct management of Mr. and Mrs. Davis from its opening date to the present time.

Ozell H. Davis completed his public schooling in Houston, Texas. He attended the Houston University--this University is now Texas Southern University.

After being honorably discharged from the U.S. Army in 1945 he entered the Texas College of Mortuary Science; after completing the course in Mortuary Science he made plans for opening Colonial Mortuary in Lufkin.

Colonial Mortuary is well known for its sympathetic and courteous ambulance and Mortuary services.

Fig. 50. Colonial Mortuary, c. 1956.
The Mirror 1955-1955-56," Negro Chamber of Commerce and Dunbar

Fig. 51. Finus Price, First Negro Blacksmith, c.1960.
Author Family Photograph
"A blacksmith operated downtown Lufkin near city hall today on Third Street. Mr. Finis Price (author's grandfather) was the only blacksmith we had in the early years."[56]

Fig. 52, Typical Blacksmith Shop, c. 1910s.
"The Village Smith," Library of Congress, D.C.

In the downtown area, there were a few Negro businesses. Charlie Gann has a restaurant near what was then called Cotton Square, near the railroad tracks. His restaurant was near the original Lufkin Library. Also, Ruby Café was right on Frank Street just as traffic came out from the underpass to the left. A cotton gin was across the railroad tracks off Abney. It dates back to the 1920s. The Daniel Hotel was next to the cotton gin.[57]

Fig. 53. Typical cotton gin, c. 1940s.
PBS

Lufkin Downtown Map c. 1930s – 1960s

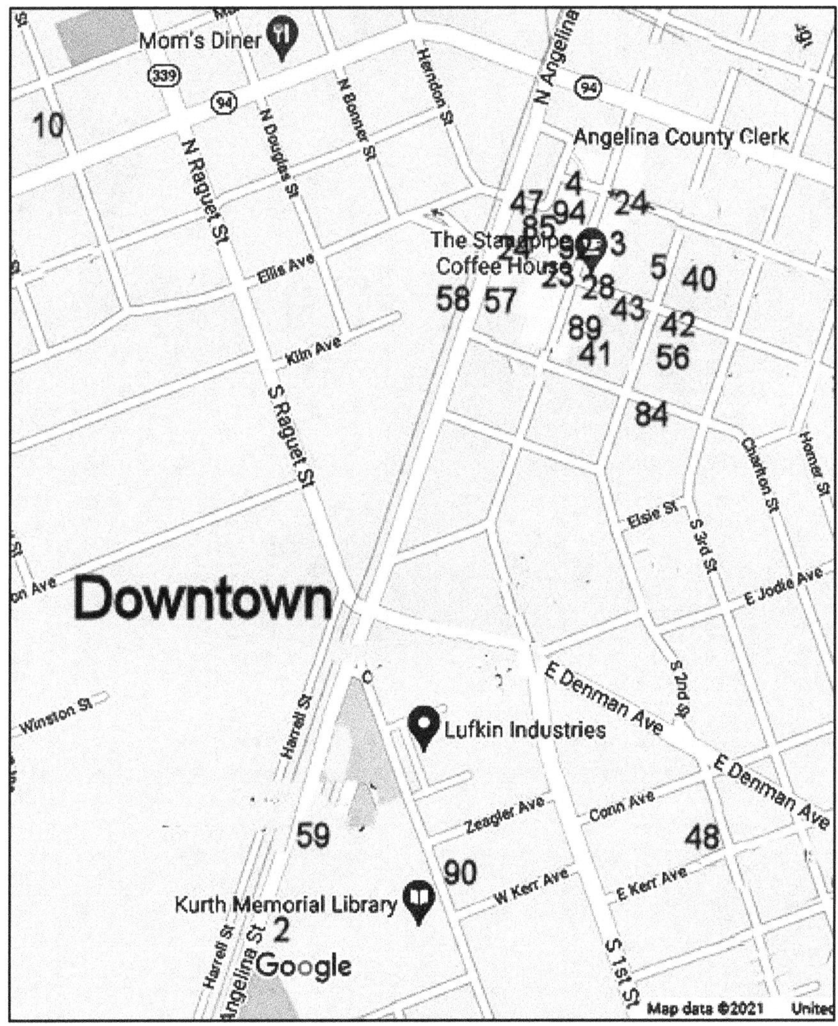

Fig. 54. Lufkin, Texas – Downtown, c. 1930s-1960s.

Google (2021) map data

Original Map using approximate site locations referenced by contemporary inhabitants

2	Lufkin Foundry & Machine	S. Angelina St & Kerr (one blk from H.E.& W.T. depot)
4	Ruby's Cafe	Frank St, just as you come out of the underpass to your left
5	Charlie Gann Restaurant	Facing library
7	Lufkin Cotton Gin, Wrecking yard/salvage	S. 3rd St, 1 blk S. of Burke Ave. Abney, across from Uncle Felix
8	Daniel Hotel	next to cotton gin, Abney
23	Former train station, then fire station	Douglass & Franklin, by the track
24	Lufkin High School	S. Raquet, SE Corner Ellis Ave
28	Lynn Theatre	Downtown Frank, 1st St
40	Finis Price, blacksmith	Downtown near City Hall, 3rd Street, 1930s), 212 Burke
41	1000 Alley Entertainment Center	Downtown 1st St & Angelina, where Lufkin Conroe Tele is now
42	Big Barber's barbershop	1000 Alley
43	Maggie McCoy beauty shop	1000 Alley
47	Buzzard Roost (Lynn Theatre)	Upper floor of Lynne Theatre
48	Texan Theatre	1st St across from Lynn Theatre
56	Pool Hall, domino shack	1000 Alley
57	Fire station	Where Kurth Library is (Douglass & Franklin), West Side Cotton Sq
58	Train station	Near where Kurth Library is, Douglass & Frankline besides the tracks on Angelina, Cotton Square, West side
59	Cotton Square	built later, where train station was. One blk west of First at the intersection of Lufkin Ave.

62	Angelina Hotel and Coffee Shop	Corner of S. First & Shepard, On Abney, Walker Quarters
84	Abney Hardware	Downtown became Cannon & Parker's
85	Harry Abram & Sons Dry Goods	112 Cotton Square, 112 S. First
89	Pine Theatre	Current location on Main st.
90	Kurth Library (current location)	709 South Raquet St., W. Kerr Ave
91	Kurth Memorial Library (original location)	Where the fire station used to be, near the train station on Douglas & Franklin besides the tracks on Angelina St.
92	Perry Brothers	104 Cotton Square

Original Map using approximate site locations referenced by contemporary inhabitants

Fig. 55. Angelina Hotel & Coffee Shop, c. 1920s.

Luftex.com

Downtown, before the war, there was a wrecking yard and a salvage yard just across Abney, right across from Uncle Felix's place. Before the salvage yard, there used to be a cotton gin. The picket factory was all on the other side.[58]

Fig. 56. King Faisal II touring a cotton gin plant, c. 1952.
Harry S. Truman Library and Museum
Inside of Typical Cotton Gin Plant

One Thousand Alley was downtown off First Street between First and Angelina, where the telephone (Lufkin Conroe Telephone) building is now.[59] It was just a block. But what a block! That one block had a barbershop, a pool hall, a taxi stand and other things. Big Barber was an early black-owned barber. Maggie McCoy also cut hair there. There was a pool hall and domino shack, too.

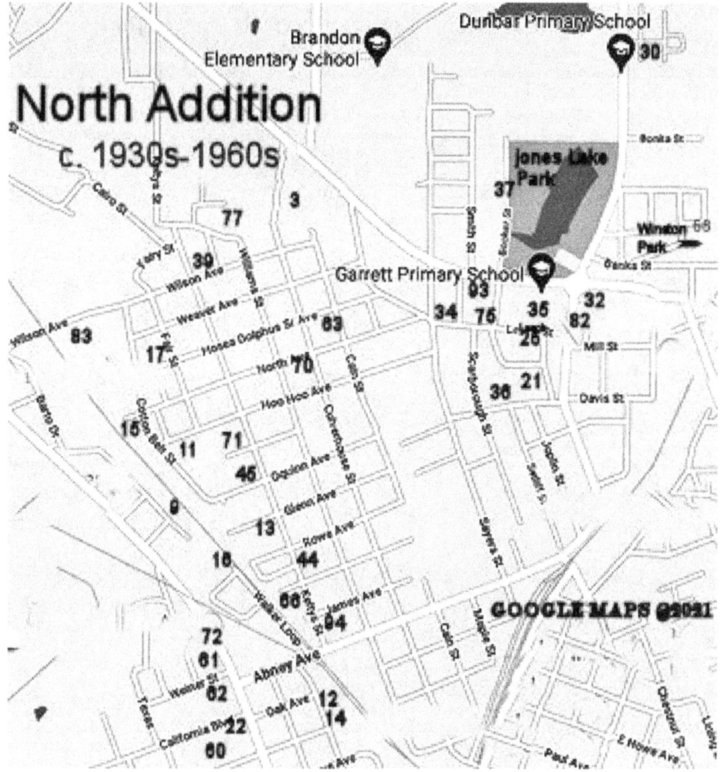

Fig. 57. Lufkin, Texas - North Addition, c. 1930s-1960s.

Google (2021) map data

Original Map using approximate site locations referenced by contemporary inhabitants

Lufkin Texas - North Addition

3	Tatum's Cleaners	1919 Wilson St
6	Uncle Felix Restaurant, Domino shack	Abney in Walker Quarters
9	Walker Quarters	Cotton belt, houses between the two rail lines that meet at Abney. Directly behind Congo Club
10	Pine Grove Hall Dance Club	Grove St
11	Church Well's Dance Hall	On Cotton belt & Keltys
12	Prof. Thomas's Café (2 story bldg	Keltys & James
13	Star Hotel	Keltys & O'Quin
15	Clyde Davis Night Club & Dance Hall	Cotton belt (near trestles) & North
16	Clyde Davis Little Ducks Night Club & Dance Hall	Walker Quarters - Cotton Belt and North
17	McClendon's Dance Club and Theatre	Wilson & Cotton Belt
21	James E. Mattox Gulf Service Station	404 Kurth Drive
22	O.E. Shelton Grocery	1022 Wilson Ave
25	First Baptist	222 Leach Ave @ Lakeview
32	Jones Park	Lakeview @ Timberland Drive
38	Pace/Tim's Funeral home	Leach St
39	New Addition/ North Lufkin	Wilson St, Kelty's St
44	Charlie Malone's Horeshoe Motel	Walker Quarters
45	Parilee Dodd barbershop	Kelty's St
60	Stephano Joseph & Son Grocery	324 N. Angelina Ave.
61	Dance Hall	Walker Quarters
63	East Tex. Cotton Club	Wilson & Culverhouse
66	Congo Club	Directly behind Walker Quarters
69	Brandon School	Keltys Drive
70	Greater Shiloh Baptist	1519 Williams St @ Hosea Dolphus Sr.Ave
71	Little Ducks End	Owned by Clyde Davis in Walkers Quarters
72	New Zion Church (Original)	North Raquet passed Abney

75	Pace Funeral Home, E.Tx. Undertaking	218 Leach St @ Lakeview
77	Horseshoe Motel	Owned by Charlie Malone near Wilson St in New Addition
81	Station One Post Office	Operated by S.T. Lewis in North Lufkin
82	Dr. S.C. Packard's clinic	On now MLK
83	Angelina Lumber	Keltys section bounded by N. Raquet St, Kurth Dr north of Abney St.
88	Geneva's Drive-In	620 Kurth Drive
93	Garrett Elementary School First Dunbar High	Current site, Leach St & Kurth Dr.
94	Lincoln Theatre owned by Joe Stefano	Keltys St, where Congo Club was located

Table 4. Site locations for North Addition

Original Map using approximate site locations referenced by contemporary inhabitants (see fig. 53.)

The New Addition was located on the corner of Wilson Street and Abney area in north Lufkin. It is called North Lufkin today. In the 1930s, it wasn't very heavily populated. However, like many other neighborhoods built for Negroes, construction was very similar. The houses were essentially two or three-room shacks. Walkers Quarters was located in New Addition off of Kelty's Street and Cotton Belt. Walker's homes were found between the two rail lines that meet at Abney directly behind Congo Club. D. H. Walker owned other properties in Lufkin during that time. He had a lot of rental houses and over that period, he also had a store and a couple of grocery stores in town. He tried to buy up all the property in this area. There was also a dance hall and a restaurant, too.

"Uncle Felix" had a domino shack in Walker Quarter. Later, Charlie Malone built the Horseshoe Motel in this area. Negro businesses flourished. That economic success gave these businesses the discretionary income to fund activities within the African American community, such as youth sports, parades and public celebrations.

Fig. 58. Charlie Williams Yankees, c. 1956.
"The Mirror 1955-56," Negro Chamber of Commerce and
Dunbar High School

There were little cafes, barbershops and a taxi stand. Parilee Dodd had her barbershop on Kelty's Street.[60]

Fig. 59. Lewis Motel & Beauty Shop, c. 1956.
"The Mirror 1955-56," Negro Chamber of Commerce and Dunbar High School

S.T. Lewis operated Station One post office. People of North Lufkin would come to the post office to get their mail because mail was not delivered to their homes. L.C. Lillie (author's uncle) had what was called the Blue Room on Chestnut. This gathering place is where the community's teenagers could gather and dance.

Dr. Charles McClendon was the first black doctor in Lufkin. After him, Dr. Simmons arrived. His practice was on Chestnut about 418 or 420. The building burned later years later. Dr. Simmons' clinic was in the lower part on the first floor of the Masonic Building on 422 Chestnut. Upstairs is where the Masonic family met.[61]

The existence of youth sports allowed the young black talents to possibly flourish and eventually have an opportunity to become the next Jackie Robinson or Willie Mays. These were underfunded leagues that got together on open fields and parks. Only the first baseman and catcher were assured of having gloves. Yet despite these shortcomings, the love of baseball was kept alive. However, it is no mystery that the demise of these neighborhoods teams in black communities eventually led to the disappearance of African American players at the major league baseball level. These children now lack the funds to participate in the AAU, Select All-Star team that travels across the country with uniforms, gear and coaching that rivals colleges.

Fig. 60. Carl Williams Yankees, c. 1956.
"The Mirror 1955-56," Negro Chamber of Commerce and Dunbar High School

Fig. 61. James Hackney Grocery Store, c. 1956.
"The Mirror 1955-56," Negro Chamber of Commerce and
Dunbar High School
Hackney's Grocery and Market. Established in 1937.
James A. Hackney, Owner.

Lufkin had several black grocers. The first black grocery store was on 408 Chestnut in the Historic District. Then came Carl Hackney's Grocery Store located at 418 Chestnut. Mr. Hackney was a forward-thinking businessman. His grocery store allowed customers to call in what they wanted and he would deliver it. Alternately, a customer could come into the store and purchase their groceries and Hackney would deliver them to their house.[62]

Fig. 62. James Hackney, c. 1956.
The Mirror 1955-56,
Negro Chamber of Commerce and Dunbar High School
Montana Lillie Neighbor on Chestnut St. c.1956

Fig. 63. Typical East Texas Diner c. 1940s
Texas Monthly

Dr. Packard was the only Lufkin black physician in the mid-forties and early fifties. He was the first black physician who was allowed to practice medicine in the local hospitals. There were two nurses at Packard's clinic. Unfortunately, his black nurses were not allowed to work at the hospital. Dr. Packard's patients, who were referred to the hospital, had to be seen by a white doctor. The hospital would not allow Dr. Packard to follow his patients into the hospital and treat them. This restrictive practice was finally broken under Dr. Allen.

Fig. 64. Dr. Samuel C. Packer, c. 1956.
"The Mirror 1955-56," Negro Chamber of Commerce and Dunbar High School
"Dr. Packer has operated the Packer Hospital Clinic, 442 Lake Street in Lufkin, since 1945."

White doctors would sometimes make house calls at black homes. But sick black people would often find it extremely challenging to schedule an available time. Many, but not all, white doctors would also see black patients in their medical clinics. Of these, Negro patients would often be seated in segregated waiting rooms. Also, restrictions of the segregated system would not permit white doctors to place their black patients in a private hospital room or even in a non-private room. They had to leave their Negro patients in the hallways. So, blacks felt that they couldn't get the best care available as white patients because the best facilities were not in the hallways.[63]

Fig. 65. Sheppard's BBQ, Est. in 1955 by G.S. Sheppard. "The Mirror 1955-56," Negro Chamber of Commerce and Dunbar High School

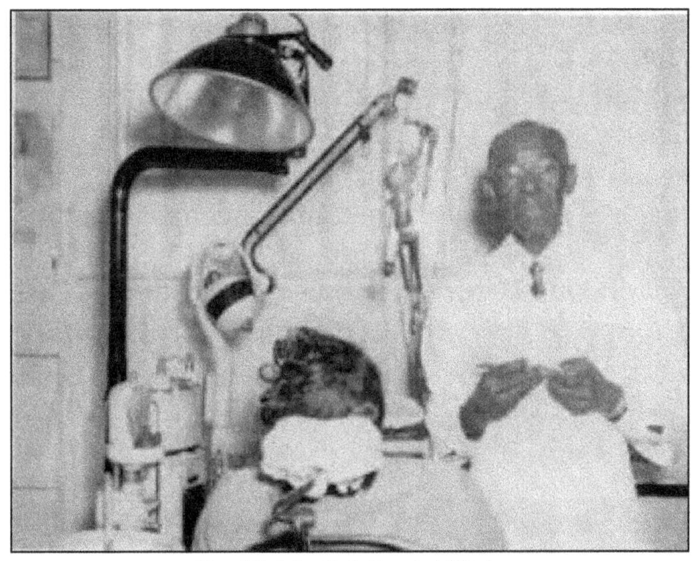

Fig. 66. Martin's Dental Clinic
Est. 1924 by Dr. J.M. Martin
"The Mirror 1955-56," Negro Chamber of Commerce and
Dunbar High School

Fig. 67. Ida V. Givens, Agent, Atlanta Life Ins.. c. 1956
"The Mirror 1955-56," Negro Chamber of Commerce and
Dunbar High School

Mrs. Givens was a member of a critical employee workforce. She was an African American working for a predominantly white organization typically dedicated to serving her community. Many blacks like her were the early leaders in white corporate America.

It was not unusual for insurance agents, county agricultural agents and salespeople of many industries to be of the same race as that individual's primary constituents. Their presence brought instant credibility and trust to an institution that the Negro community might not have previously dealt with before.

Fig. 68. House's Cafe, Est. 1943, c. 1956.
"The Mirror 1955-56," Negro Chamber of Commerce and Dunbar High School

Fig. 69. William & Son Grocery, Est. 1937.
"The Mirror 1955-56," Negro Chamber of Commerce and
Dunbar High School
Carl Williams Owner, c. 1956.

Fig. 70. East Tx Undertaking, Est. 1926.
"The Mirror 1955-56," Negro Chamber of Commerce and
Dunbar High School
I.D. Tims Owner c. 1956

Tims Funeral Home had its beginning in 1928. Its founder was the late Mr. L.S. Pace, who was also an educator in the public schools of Lufkin. He named the business East Texas Funeral Home and that name stood for more than 30 years. Mr. Pace sold the funeral home to the late I.D. and Opal Tims in the late 1940s. It was located at 224 Leach Street, next door to the First Missionary Baptist Church. It occupied the lower floor of the Prince Hall Masonic Lodge Building. Around 1960, Tims purchased a local church sanctuary and moved the funeral home adjacent to the Lodge Hall at 222 Leach. The name was changed during the dedication to Tims Funeral Home.[64]

Fig. 71. Inez Tims, Influential Local Leader, c. 1956.
"The Mirror 1955-56," Negro Chamber of Commerce and Dunbar High School

Fig. 72. Slim Jenkins' Garage, Est. 1948.

"The Mirror 1955-56," Negro Chamber of Commerce and
Dunbar High School
D.J. Jenkins Owner

Fig. 73, Gulf Service Station, Est. 1954.
James E. Mattox Owner

Fig. 74. Geneva's Drive-In, c. 1956.
"The Mirror 1955-56," Negro Chamber of Commerce and
Dunbar High School
Geneva Brown Owner,
"Located 620 Kurth Drive, opened May 6, 1954."

Fig. 75. Universal Life Ins., A.H. Carlton, c. 1964.
"Tiger 64," Dunbar High School Annual
910 Cain Street

It is sad to note that none of these businesses seemed to have survived desegregation. Apparently, as their core cliental were given the opportunity to spend their dollars anywhere, they spent it increasingly more in the former whites-only establishments. Perhaps the minimally capitalized black-owned businesses could not afford to fund modern improvements such as air-conditioning or new health and safety codes. The reasons for their demise are beyond the scope of this book. But its implications and ramifications are being felt today.

9

Cornerstone Employers

Fig. 76, Lufkin Foundry, c. 1956.
"The Mirror 1955-56," Negro Chamber of Commerce and
Dunbar High School

"THE LUFKIN FOUNDRY AND MACHINE COMPANY of Lufkin, Texas (c.1956) is recognized as one of the largest manufacturing concerns in the South. And yet it had its beginning as a small sawmill machinery repair shop. THE GROWTH of this Company from a few employees when it was found-ed in 1902, to its present employment of more than 1300 persons is explained by its only surviving founder in a few words. MR. W. C. TROUT, the late beloved President of this Company for many years, joined the Lufkin Foundry in 1905, and soon Lufkin's name appeared in sawmills throughout East Texas, Arkansas, and Louisiana. In 1923, Lufkin installed their first geared pumping unit at Goose Creek, Texas. OF THIS COMPANY was happy to have had a large financial share in

the civic program to pave streets in the Negro section of Lufkin, and in the effort to provide better housing facilities for the colored people of Lufkin. THE LUFKIN FOUNDRY AND MACHINE COMPANY salutes the Negroes of Angelina County, and pledges its support to their endeavors to raise and maintain their high standard of living."

In the 1960s, major employers like Lufkin Industries or Texas Foundry allocated funds to assist their Negro employees to build some houses. Until that effort was made, it was very difficult for blacks to get home loans because they lacked sufficient assets to secure a loan. After that time, blacks with jobs were not considered at high risk for default. Banks saw that blacks could be dependable and beneficial borrowers just like their white working counterparts.[65]

The Lufkin Foundry statement from their leadership printed in 1956 demonstrates the prevailing attitude of the times of even the most reputable businesses of the time. There was an odd incongruence of exhibiting benevolence toward Negroes while still operating in a deeply segregated society.

"Of the more than 1300 employees of this Company, some 225 are Negro employees. Lufkin Foundry is proud of its Negro employees. They are good citizens, taking an active part in the Negro Chamber of Commerce, the Negro Division of the Community Chest, and the activities of the Negro Public Schools." **1956 Mirror**

Fig. 77. Texas Foundry, c. 1956.
"The Mirror 1955-56," Negro Chamber of Commerce and
Dunbar High School

Texas Foundries, Inc. became a reality because several men from St. Louis recognized a need in East Texas for a malleable iron Foundry. The new company was organized and chartered on October 31, 1938. As of Jan 1, 1956, Texas Foundries - employed 575 people.

Texas Foundries, Inc. purchased the Southern Malleable Iron Company assets in exchange for stock. The equipment, patterns, and other East St. Louis foundry assets were bought and moved to the new company. The first president of Texas Foundries was W.C. Trout. Texas Foundries devoted almost all production from 1942 - 1945 to WWII orders. Foundry production jobs were modified to permit women to replace men who had been drafted.

Texas Foundry made pump units for the oil field and smaller iron parts for the war. The old foundry had begun to make guns for the war. They already made smaller equipment for ship parts. Many jobs were made available for African Americans during this hyper-growth period. Brakemen needed a high school education, but many new jobs at the Foundry only required the strength and desire to endure a harsh work environment. Unfortunately, access to many better-paying jobs remained restricted to whites only. Blacks weren't allowed to operate the machine where they dressed the casting and carried it into the machine shop. But they would be allowed to teach a white person how to operate the same machine.[66]

Allegedly, Inez Tims led a legal battle that got many job restrictions lifted for Negroes. Many believed that Tims was responsible for blacks working in the local banks. His leadership ability and respected position in the community led to him becoming President of the Black Chamber of Commerce in Lufkin in the 1940s. That was the time when many local Negroes felt many things started to change for Negroes.[67]

The author's father, Clark Jackson Price, son of blacksmith Finus Price and son-in-law of the Architect's worker Montana Lillie, started working at Texas Foundry shortly after dropping out of high school. He continued working there until his untimely death from a brain tumor in 1968. There are vivid memories of him coming home every night blackened by the soot at the foundry. He had a job that placed him in some of the dirtiest, hottest areas of the facility. At times, it seemed that there was black soot oozing from his skin even after a daily bath. Despite his physical challenges, Clark managed to go to work every day. While he never earned more than $130 a week, he did manage to feed his family of six.

FIVE TO TEN YEARS: Front Row, left to right: A. Z. Handy, Joe Jackson, L. C. Wagner, Marell McClendon, Perkins Johnson, Fred Reynolds, Henry Lewis, Ernest Spikes, Wren Topps, Leslie Frazier, John W. Sapp; Second Row, left to right: Clyde Lewis, Bernard Austin, George Connor, George Collins, Jr., Johnny McClendon, Green Woods, Jr., Henry Dixon, M. R. Polk, Mossye Handy, Dan Roundtree, Cleo Cartwright; Third Row, left to right: Clarence Horace, Willie D. Colquitt, Glenn Gamble, James D. Fears, John L. Moore, Ben J. Collins, W. G. Gasaway,, Manuel Rhodes, Lester Johnson, Edgar Hardin, Columbus Deckard; Fourth Row, left to right: R. Q. Forney, Mack Keggler, Wade D. Johnson, Jeffrey Collier, Clark J. Price, Winfred Caldwell, Frank Lively, Lonnie Reynolds, Batie Deason, Eddie Shepherd, Monroe Cilder, Damon Denman. Not Present: James Mattox, Jim Ikner, Ottis Jackson, Robert D. Johnson, James McCraw, John H. Moore, Leonard Morris, Haywood Singleton, Vater Tatum, Alton Buckley, Clome Finley, James Hagens, Earnest Jackson, Herbert Davis, Jimmie Whitaker, Buster Traylor, Maurell Handy, Johnnie Jones, Emmett Thompson, Roscoe Jackson, Nahala Johnson, Robert Miller, Lonnie B. Sparks, Rubin Gardner, Grose Kiel, Jack Washington, Willie Coleman.

Fig. 78. Texas Foundry Employees, c. 1956.

"The Mirror 1955-56," Negro Chamber of Commerce and Dunbar High School
Including the author's father, Clark J. Price

Fig. 79. Texas Foundry Negro Employees, c. 1955.
(Author's family photograph)

Fig. 80. Southland Paper Mills, c. 1956.
"The Mirror 1955-56," Negro Chamber of Commerce and
Dunbar High School

The official Southland Papermill Management statement concerning their historic beginnings: *"In 1936, when newsprint production was on the decline in the U.S. Mills, consideration was given by industrial leads and publishers in the south to the feasibility of manufacturing newsprint from southern pine. Dr. Charles Herty and the late Francis Gawan carried out experimental work over a long period of time which provides that it was possible and practical to make newsprint from southern pine. In January 1940, the first newsprint made commercially from southern pine was produced at this mill."* **The Mirror**

The 1940s were full of change as Lufkin's prosperity continued to grow on the backs of lumber and steel. As the WWII war effort grew, the foundries were at full capacity making guns, tanks and other war machinery.

10
Churches

Unlike the fate of most, if not all, of the African American-owned businesses of this time, the Black Church has endured. Though aged or remodeled, many churches featured remain in the community today.

Its enduring presence is no surprise. Black Churches throughout the South have been involved in every aspect of the Negro community since shortly after slavery. It has been in the foreground in the fight for civil rights, education and economic growth and preservation of the African American culture.

Through it all, African Americans have drawn strength through faith and the opportunity to gather together.

Fig. 81. New Zion Baptist Church, c. 1920s.

Fig. 82. New Zion Baptist Church, c. 1940s.
"The Mirror 1955-56," Negro Chamber of Commerce and Dunbar
High School
The church was remodeled with additional improvements and parking

Fig. 83. Goodwill Baptist Church, original, c. 1900.

Fig. 84. Goodwill Baptist Church (new), c. 1921
"The Mirror 1955-56," Negro Chamber of Commerce and
Dunbar High School
Organized in 1898 by Rev. G. A. Bowman and others.
One of the churches that Montana Lillie assisted Will Ingram to
build

The Goodwill Baptist Church was organized in 1898 by Rev. G. A. Bowman and others. The first site was in the Old Lufkin Land addition. The second church was built on the Clark and Chestnut site in 1912. It was torn down and the present church was built there in May 1921. Rev. A. D. Thomas served faithfully from 1944 to 1979.[68]

Fig. 85. First Baptist Church, c. 1912.
"The Mirror 1955-56," Negro Chamber of Commerce and Dunbar High School

First Baptist Church was organized in 1900 in the old Masonic Hall in the Sherral Addition by Rev. Andrew Mitchell. It was named Pilgrim Rest Baptist Church. The first members were Rev. George Bowman (and Will Ingram). Pilgrim Rest Baptist Church burned in 1912 and the group worshipped in a tabernacle where the parsonage now sits. The church was rebuilt in 1912, a short while after it (too) burned and (the new church) was named "First Baptist Church." Rev. Joe James became pastor in 1925 and under his leadership, the present First Baptist Church was built.[69]

Fig. 86. Mt. Calvary Baptist Church
Keltys, Texas (Now part of Lufkin)
Mt. Calvary Baptist Church was organized in Keltys on May 7, 1892. Rev. J.J. James was

Fig. 87. Shiloh Baptist Church

"The Mirror 1955-56," Negro Chamber of Commerce and Dunbar High School.

Shiloh Baptist Church is located on the corner of Highland and Williams back of Brandon Elementary school. It was organized in 1927. The church was rebuilt in 1953 when the old structure was sold to the Lufkin Public School System

Fig. 88. Long Chapel C.M.E. Church, c. 1946.

"The Mirror 1955-56," Negro Chamber of Commerce and Dunbar High School

Long Chapel C.M.E. Church was organized in 1892 by Father Mims on the old Squire Long Property. M. Johnson built the present church in 1908. On August 12, 1946, the current building was erected by Rev.

Squire Long was one of the founders of the Masonic Lodge on Beech Street in 1893. He owned 100 acres of land where Al Myer Ford now stands. Long Chapel CME is named after him. He gave the property for the first church at the end of Groesbeck, where it meets Chestnut Street.[70]

Fig. 89. West End of God in Christ.

"The Mirror 1955-56," Negro Chamber of Commerce and Dunbar High School

The Church of God in Christ is located in the nine hundred block on Nile Street. The description of the church is brown brick and a two-story building. The church was established in 1945.

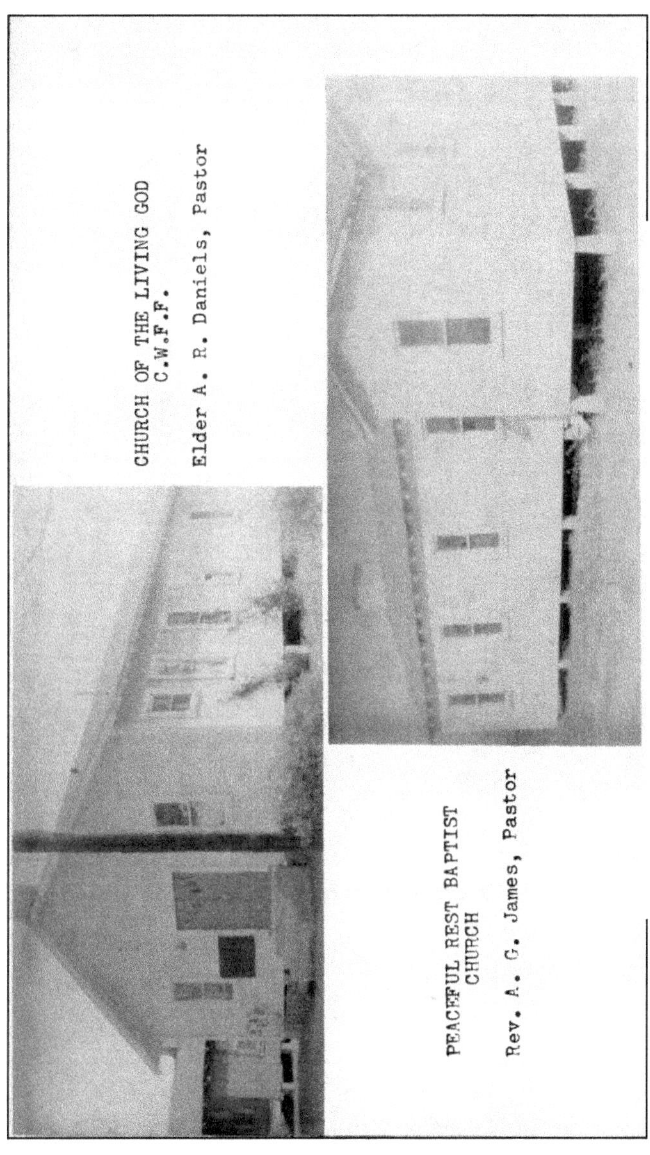

Fig. 90. Other Lufkin Area Negro Churches. "The Mirror 1955-56," Negro Chamber of Commerce and Dunbar High School

Fig. 91. Other Negro Churches.

"The Mirror 1955-56," Negro Chamber of Commerce and Dunbar High School

Other Lufkin Area Negro Churches Continued

Historical Map of Lufkin, circa 1940s

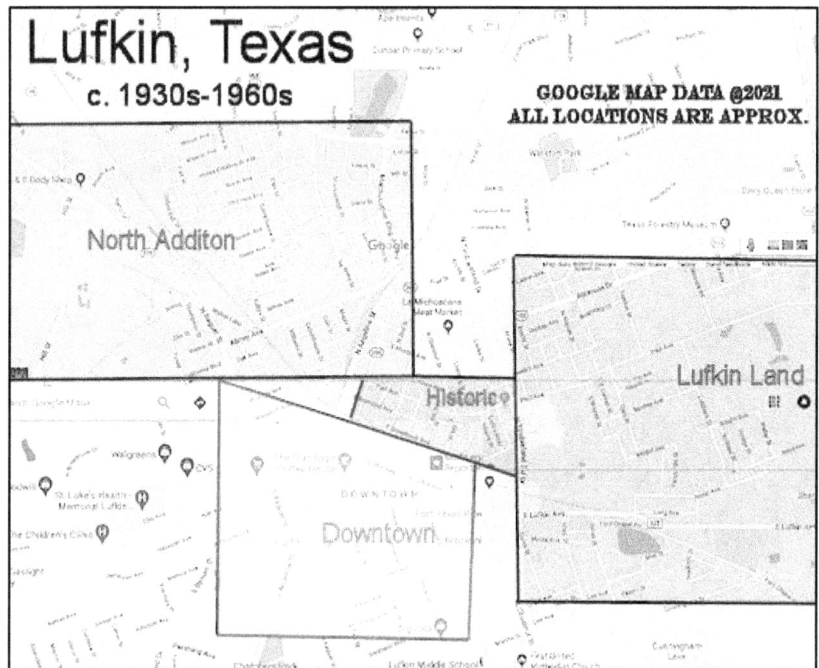

Fig. 92. Lufkin, Texas, c. 1930s - 1960s.
Google Map Data
Created by the Author

11
Grade Schools

County school records rarely mentioned Negro schools. There is great difficulty finding records or formal discussions of Negro schools. [71] Consequently, most of the images, discussions and events displayed in the school chapters have been generated or provided by African Americans of that era.

Fig. 93. G.W. Carver Elementary
"Tiger 64," Dunbar High School Annual

Carver Elementary School was constructed in 1939-40. Later, Carver was rebuilt (off Chestnut Street) in 1964. Mrs. Olivia Hackney was the Principal of the original Carver. During the dedication of the new Carver, the school was named in her honor.

While the quality of education for Lufkin Negro students is and will be discussed in this book and elsewhere, it should not be forgotten that children will be children. The quality of education is not solely based on books, test tubes and facilities. Education also provides a profoundly meaningful opportunity for children to be children, for people of all ages to learn how to work together and for the imagination to soar, thinking about the possibilities ahead.

Fig. 94. First Graders Carver Elementary, c. 1956.
"The Mirror 1955-56," Negro Chamber of Commerce and Dunbar High School

Fig. 95. Olivia R. Hackney Principal
"Tiger 64," Dunbar High School Annual

Lufkin Independent School District has had a wonderful tradition of naming predominantly black schools after local African American Pioneer educators. Names like Brandon, Garrett and Hackney should form the basis of a lasting legacy.

Fig. 96. Brandon Elementary School
"Tiger 64," Dunbar High School Annual
Brandon was built c. 1923

Fig. 97. Original Melinda Garret Elementary School
"Tiger 64," Dunbar High School Annual

Norris and Malinda Garrett donated the land on which the original Dunbar was built. The location later became the site for Malinda Garrett Elementary School, which was named in Garett's honor.

Fig. 98. Melinda Garrett
"Tiger 64," Dunbar High School Annual
Garrett Elementary School Administrator

Fig. 99. Third Grade, c. 1956
"The Mirror 1955-56," Negro Chamber of Commerce and
Dunbar High School

Fig. 100. Newer Garrett Elementary School
"Tiger 64," Dunbar High School Annual

Fig. 101. Cedar Grove Elementary
"Tiger 64," Dunbar High School Annual
Located in North Lufkin

12
High Schools

History of Lufkin High Schools for African Americans

LUCKY WARD COLORED SCHOOL
NORTH CHESTNUT ST.
1905-1923

On November 5, 1903, the Chapman family Lots 3 and 4 of the Chapman Addition part of the Quinalty League in Lufkin, Texas, was sold to Austin Garrett, Sidney Hackney and Squire Long Trustees of the Colored School District No. 2. This sale on Chestnut Street in the Historic District made it possible to open the Lucky Ward Negro School. [72]

Lucky Ward became the first high school for Negroes in Lufkin. The school was operational sometime between the years 1903 and 1923. The author speculates that the Lucky Ward School opened on a site where most structures were already built. Prior title transfers indicated previous owners included Dr. D. S. Simmons and the Masonic Lodge. Unsubstantiated family lore by Montana Lillie stated that he had helped build or remodel the building. (This is the building that he eventually purchased as his home.) Also, there were stories that the building had been a Doctor's office, barbershop and rent homes before his purchase in 1929.

Fig. 102. Lucky Ward School, c. 1920-1923
Museum of East Texas Collections
First Negro High School in Lufkin

"There were two Negro schools in Lufkin before Dunbar. The Kelty's school. The other was the Lucky Ward School located on North Chestnut." Angelina County Historical Commission

Fig. 103. Lucky Ward Graduating Class, c. 1920s
Museum of East Texas Collections, Lufkin, Tx

Fig. 104. Lucky Ward Faculty, c. 1920s.
Museum of East Texas Collections.
Members of the Lucky Ward Faculty. [73]

ORIGINAL DUNBAR HIGH SCHOOL
LEACH STREET
1923-1951

The school term 1923-24 was a period for the beginning of a new school location for the Black people of Lufkin.

The new school was a six-room stucco building located on Leach Street administered by one principal, three teachers and the students from the old Lucky Ward School. At first, the school taught grades primary through nine. Later they added tenth grade and eventually expanded to include grades eleven and twelve. The principal was N. C. Brandon. The teachers were Mmes. Malinda Garrett, Minnie B. Johnson and Annie (Henry) Penson.[74]

A persistent story circulated within the African American community that Mrs. Malinda Garrett and her husband, Austin Garrett, donated the land on Leach Street for the new school. Their actions were due to their intense desire for a good school building for Lufkin's black children. The validity of that claim could not be verified, but it is consistent with her passion for education.

The students who first moved into the new school building from Lucky Ward were given the privilege to name the school. They chose the name Paul Lawrence Dunbar (1872 – 1906) in honor of the great writer who was one of the most popular poets of his time and the first Black American writer to achieve a national and international reputation.[75]

The school's opening promised a new era in Negro education in Lufkin.

My rose began to open, and its hue
Was sweet to me as to it sun and dew;
I watched it taking on its ruddy flame
Until the day of perfect blooming came,
Then hasted I with smiles to find it blushing red — Too late!
Some thoughtless child had plucked my rose and fled!
PROMISE by Paul Lawrence Dunbar[76]

Fig. 105. Dunbar High School, c.1924.
"The Mirror 1955-56," Negro Chamber of Commerce and
Dunbar High School
Original Dunbar High School (1924-1952)
Dunbar replaced Lucky Ward as the high school for blacks in
Lufkin

In the spring of 1924, N. C. Branon resigned from Dunbar and
when the fall term began in 1924, W. H. Brandon was named
Principal. Brandon was a dynamic educator who believed that
the whole child should be developed.[77]

Fig. 106. William Brandon, c. 1956.
"The Mirror 1955-56," Negro Chamber of Commerce and
Dunbar High School

Although the Curriculum was limited and very few books were provided, Professor Brandon (Fess) taught science with rocks, soil, leaves, sticks, and other readily available items. A student of the Class of 1931 - recalls having the students purchase a small Mathematics book for further study of the subject due to the inadequacy of the books provided by the school district. A student in the Class of 1935 remembers Brandon teaching them geometry. This subject was not yet a course in the curriculum at that time. Brandon felt it was necessary to introduce the topic to ensure a well-rounded education. Another course taught by Brandon was grammar.[78]

Some of the earliest Graduates included[79] :

First Graduating Dunbar Class (circa 1928)
Hester Austin
Fannie Castle
Lottie Jackson
Mable Jackson
Freddie Johnson
Leroy Lewis

Dunbar Class of 1929
Annie Mae Flowers
Geneva Johnson
Velma Washington
Ellis Carrington
Evie B. Kegler
Vera Blake Morris Richards
Rosie Bell Garrett
Ora Lee Jackson
Lucius Williams
Lewis Durden

Fig. 107. Dunbar High School Faculty, c. 1934.
"Tiger 64," Dunbar High School Annual

Even though Dunbar was an improvement over Lucky Ward, there were still other opportunities at Lufkin High that Dunbar did not experience. There were no foreign language classes. The only science class (which opened in the fall of 1936) offered a biology class with a little workbook that students worked through. There was no science equipment, no supplies or much of anything else except a Bunsen burner and a flask.[80]

The science courses taught at Dunbar were general science and physics. As subject matter increased, additional grades were added. The eleventh grade was added in 1930 and the twelfth grade was added in 1941.

The only books that Dunbar received were those that had gone out for adoption that the white students had already used.

"By the time we got the books, there were a dozen or so names in them that had used them years before and half the pages were missing. You might be reading a story or reading a historical event on page 122 and the next page is 171, so all of that in-between you just have to imagine what transpired. We were supposed to be on par with everybody else. No way! "[81]

"Two school systems, even though it had the same name, totally two different worlds."[82] **– Rhodes**

Dunbar struggled to provide a sufficiently diverse foundational education system that would provide its graduates an easier opportunity to pursue future careers.

Many African Americans were not convinced that the school board was sufficiently committed to providing an, although separate, but equal education for the black children in public schools. There might have been a black teacher specializing in agriculture, yet they might have that person teaching English or History. Understandably they knew virtually nothing about teaching English or History. *"But it seemed that the school system leadership just wanted some live body in that room so that they could say we have somebody teaching these blacks something."*[83]

"The Lufkin Independent School District maintains the best school system in the county." –I.A. Coston, Superintendent Lufkin ISD[84]

Fig. 108. F.W. Thomas Dunbar Principal, 1943-44.
"The Dunbar Tiger," Pictorial Edition, Nov. 1943.

On Friday afternoons, twice per month, the entire student body assembled for an activity called "Literary Society." Students presented readings, poems, music (vocals and instrumental) and debates.[85]

Before 1932, the only sport in which the students engaged was basketball and the game was played out of doors. The school had no gymnasium or auditorium. All school openings, closings, assemblies, class dramas, commencement exercises and junior and senior banquets were held in the First Baptist Church, across the street from Dunbar.[86]

"Basketball conditions were worst because the Negroes were not allowed to use the white gym. They had to play basketball on dirt courts. When it rained, those dirt courts turned into mud. This was particularly restrictive in Lufkin as other area East Texas towns like Nacogdoches, Diboll and Apple Springs allowed blacks to use their indoor gyms."[87]

Negro parents in Lufkin had been requesting a school gymnasium for many years. The old Dunbar High School on Leach never had a gym. The lack of a gym was extremely frustrating when they knew many little schools in the area like Chester, Oak Ridge and several others in poor communities had gymnasiums. So, there was great excitement when plans were disclosed to build a true high school with its own gym.

"You can play out there in the cold. I can recall that on a couple of occasions it was so cold playing outside that we had to play in shifts. We literally played basketball in shifts. One would play for about five or ten minutes until everybody froze to death. [The others] were inside getting warm and then they would run out there and play for five or ten minutes until they were about froze to death and then they would come back and warm up and thaw out and we would run back out there. " **Rhodes**

In the fall of 1932, Dunbar school had its first football team and its first hired coach, Develous Johnson. The football games were played on Friday afternoons on the grounds of the Stroud Mill, located North East of U.S. Highway 35 (now U.S. Highway 59 North). The second coach was George E. Spencer, 1935-36.[88]

"I can recall our football equipment. We never got any new football equipment. The only equipment we got was the equipment that Lufkin High School threw away and that went for shoes, helmets, pads and everything yet."[89] **Kuyendall**

In the fall of 1936, C.L. Franklin, Sr., became the coach. His career was interrupted by World War II. In September 1942, Franklin enlisted into the Armed Forces to serve his country and returned to his teaching position in 1945.[90]

Fig. 109. W.R. Smith, Dunbar Football Head Coach
"The Dunbar Tiger," Pictorial Edition, Nov. 1943.

When Franklin served his country, Willie Ray Smith was employed as the Coach from 1942 to 1945.[91]

Fig. 110. Dunbar District Champions, 1943-44.
"The Dunbar Tiger," Pictorial Edition, Nov. 1943

"In the early days the Dunbar football team was allowed to play at the White Panther Stadium. Regardless of the rain, heat or snow, when the game was over the Negro players had to leave because they were not allowed to use the locker rooms and showers. They had to go back to the parking lot and change clothes in the cars. If it was a dance afterward, they put those dance clothes over their smelly bodies."[92]

Fig. 111. Dunbar Football Team, 1939
"The Mirror 1955-56," Negro Chamber of Commerce and Dunbar High School

The Dunbar sports teams could not use the school buses like the other white schools. They could only use Lufkin ISD buses when they traveled to their two longest away games in Paris and Wichita Falls, Texas (a 650-mile round trip). The other times Dunbar had to rent a truck with a canvas top in the back. The truck was usually meant to carry cattle. Even the pep squad with clean, nicely pressed uniforms had to ride in the cattle trucks.

Fig. 112. Dunbar Pep Squad Leaders, 1943-44.
"The Dunbar Tiger," Pictorial Edition, Nov. 1943.
(Vera Lillie is the author's mother)

"The situation was a degrading experience for which most blacks considered was the reason why the whites did it." **Rhodes**

Fig. 113. Typical Flatbed Truck, c.1930.
Kim Loeb Collection
1930s cattle trucks were often used to transport Negro sports teams in Lufkin

Dunbar High School was undeterred by these obstacles. Remarkably their history of athletic excellence matched or exceeded their white counterparts.

Fig. 114. Dunbar Basketball Team of 1938
"The Mirror 1955-56," Negro Chamber of Commerce and Dunbar High School

Fig. 115. Dunbar Leadership, 1943-44.
"The Dunbar Tiger," Pictorial Edition, Nov. 1943

Dunbar had its first band in the fall of 1939. Melvin
McClendon, a blind musician, gave his time to teaching
students interested in band music and could purchase their
instruments.[93]

MISS BERTHA MAE HILL
Miss Dunbar, 1943-'44

Fig. 116. Miss Dunbar, 1943-44
"The Dunbar Tiger," Pictorial Edition, Nov. 1943.
(Berta Hill is the author's aunt)

The first band members were: Chauncey Martin, Herman O'Quinn, Jr, Le Edward Charlton, Ernest B. McGowan, Ernestine Boone, Odessa Allen, Gussie Dean Tippett, Altha Martin and Billie Jean Garrett.[94]

Fig. 117. Dunbar High School Band, c.1956.
"The Mirror 1955-1955-56," Negro Chamber of

DUNBAR HIGH SCHOOL
LAKE STREET
1951 - 1970

In 1951, a new Dunbar High School was built at 1806 Lake Street (later changed to Martin Luther King Jr. Blvd). It was a modern building with a science laboratory, library, cafeteria, band hall, agriculture building, homemaking building and a field house.[95]

Fig. 118. English Departments., c. 1964.
"Tiger 64," Dunbar High School Annual

Once the new Dunbar High school was built, the old school on Leach Street became known as Garrett Elementary. It was named for Malinda Garret, one of its first teachers and the possible land donor. [96]

Fig. 119. M.E.Lyons Dunbar Principal, 1959-1968
"The Dunbar Tiger," Pictorial Edition, Nov. 1943.

Dunbar High School operated under the administration of seven principals. They were: N. C. Branon, 1923-1924; W. H. Brandon, 1924-1940; F. W. Thomas 1940-1946; J. T. Washington, Sr. 1946-1955; E.E. Cleaver 1955-1959; M. E. Lyons, 1959-1968; and Travis Carter, 1968-1970.[97]

Fig. 120. Student Safety Patrol, c.1956.
"The Mirror 1955-56," Negro Chamber of Commerce and Dunbar High School

Fig. 121. New Dunbar High School, c. 1952.
"Tiger 64," Dunbar High School Annual
1952 – 1970

In the fall of 1953, C. L. Franklin, Sr., became principal of Garrett Elementary. Elmer G. Redd was employed as a coach. He remained until Dunbar high school was phased out in 1970 due to the integration of Lufkin Independent School District's schools. Dunbar football team's journey to equality took them from the team traveling in Robert Denum flatbed trucks to ultimately on Trailway passenger buses and from winning a few games each year to winning multiple State Championships.[98]

Fig. 122. Dunbar Football Coaching Staff, 1964.
"Tiger 64," Dunbar High School Annual

Coach Redd led the Dunbar High school athletic program from 1953 through 1970. During his tenure at Dunbar, his football team won 146 games, lost 36 and tied 3. During Coach Redd's time as head football coach at Dunbar, the Tigers won three PVIL state championships and were runner-up twice. Coach Redd established one of the longest winning streaks in Texas schoolboy football history when his team won 39 games without a loss or tie. The boys' track team was District Champions 12 times between 1953 and 1967. They won the State Championship twice, in 1964 and 1967. The girls' track team was State Champions three times between 1962 and 1966.[99]

Fig. 123. 1930 Track Team
"The Mirror 1955-56," Negro Chamber of Commerce and
Dunbar High School

Despite all of Dunbar's State titles, the state governing body for white sports, the University Interscholastic League (UIL), refused to recognize black champions during this era. Black sports were administered by the Prairie View Interscholastic League (PVIL). PVIL *"played a leading role in developing African American students in the arts, literature, athletics and music"* from the 1920s through 1967. During this period, the PVIL served as the recognized governing body for extra-curricular activities for African American high schools in Texas. They were originally called the Texas Interscholastic League of Colored Schools.[100]

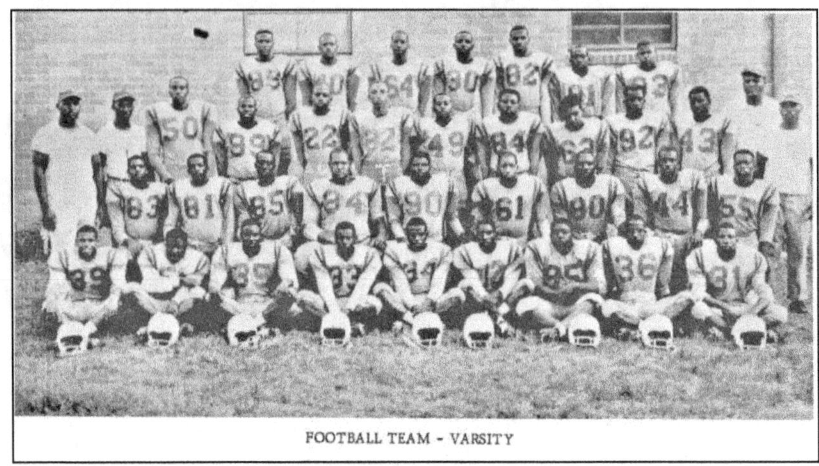

Fig. 124. Varsity Football Team, 1964.
"Tiger 64," Dunbar High School Annual

The move to merge the two leagues began on October 14, 1964, when Dr. Howard A. Calkins of the UIL State Executive Committee introduced and the full committee approved a motion urging the Legislative Council to remove the word "white" as a school membership requirement. On June 9, 1965, the UIL State Executive Committee validated the Legislative Council's decision to open league membership to all public schools. The PVIL began to merge with the UIL for the 1967-68 school year. Ultimately PVIL was disbanded at the end of the 1969-70 school year.[101]

Fig. 125. Dunbar Tennis Team, 1964.

"Tiger 64," Dunbar High School Annual

Girls- finished State Runner-up Girls' singles, District Girls' Doubles Champion, State Girls' Doubles Champion, Runner-up Scholastic National Championship
Boys - District Boys' Singles and Doubles Champion and State runner-up Singles and Doubles.

Yet, the plight of recognizing Dunbar's athletic excellence was not complete. The state championship trophies were on display for many years at Lufkin High School. At some point, they were removed. In the late 1980s, *"a cleaning crew was working at Garrett Elementary School and found Dunbar trophies in a room from Lufkin High school in water, broken, those kinds of things."* - **Kennedy**

Fig. 126. Girls' Track Team, 1964.
"Tiger 64," Dunbar High School Annual

Unfortunately, some of the Dunbar Championship plaques and trophies were never found. What remained was relocated to the former Dunbar High School to be displayed and appreciated by future generations. [102]

Fig. 127. Girls' Track Team
"The Mirror 1955--56," Negro Chamber of Commerce and
Dunbar High School

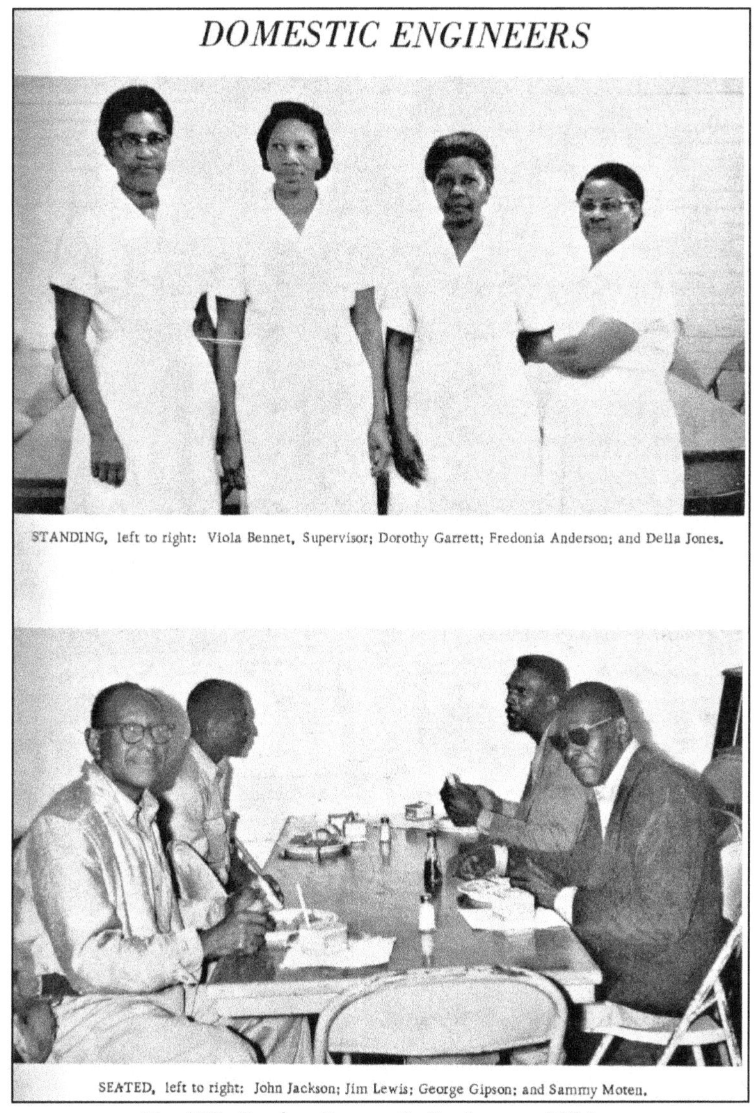

Fig. 128. Dunbar Domestic Engineers, 1964.
"Tiger 64," Dunbar High School Annual

In 1962, the Dunbar High School campus expanded with the construction of Dunbar Junior High.

Fig. 129, Miss Dunbar, 1964.
"Tiger 64," Dunbar High School Annual

The Dunbar High Senior building was constructed on one side of the road and the Junior High school was built across the street. Both schools shared the same gymnasium and cafeteria.

Fig. 130. Lufkin Dunbar Jr. High
"Tiger 64," Dunbar High School Annual
Built Across Denman Av.e from the High School.

Fig. 131. Dunbar Library
"The Mirror 1955-56," Negro Chamber of Commerce and Dunbar High School

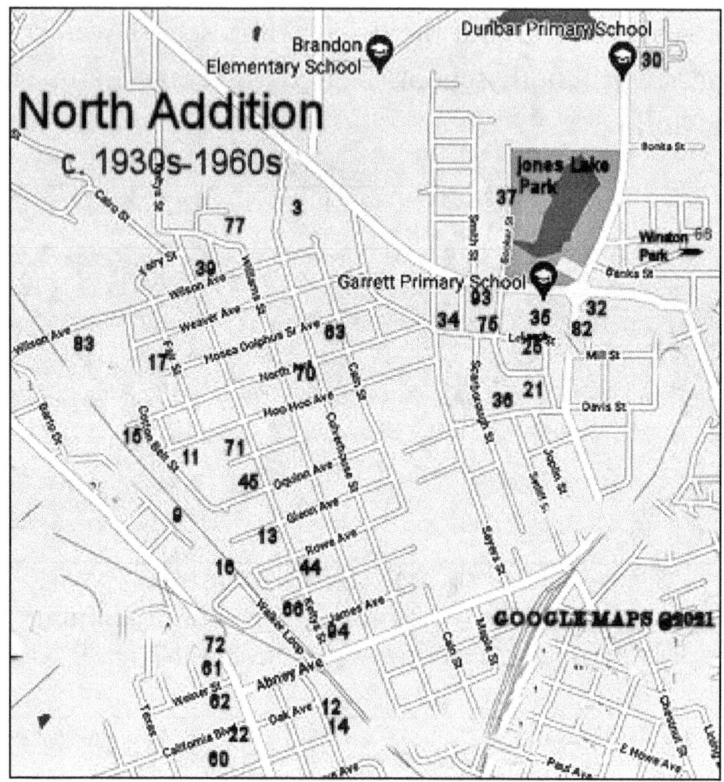

Fig. 132. Lufkin, Texas - North Addition
Google @2021 map data
Original Map using approximate site locations referenced by contemporary inhabitants

3	Tatum's Cleaners	1919 Wilson St
6	Uncle Felix Restaurant, Domino shack	Abney in Walker Quarters
9	Walker Quarters	Cotton belt, houses between the two rail lines that meet at Abney. Directly behind Congo Club
10	Pine Grove Hall Dance Club	Grove St
11	Church Well's Dance Hall	On Cotton belt & Keltys
12	Prof. Thomas's Café (2 story bldg	Keltys & James
13	Star Hotel	Keltys & O'Quin
15	Clyde Davis Night Club & Dance Hall	Cotton belt (near trestles) & North
16	Clyde Davis Little Ducks Night Club & Dance Hall	Walker Quarters - Cotton Belt and North
17	McClendon's Dance Club & Theatre	Wilson & Cotton Belt
21	James E. Mattox Gulf Service Station	404 Kurth Drive
22	O.E. Shelton Grocery	1022 Wilson Ave
25	First Baptist	222 Leach Ave @ Lakeview
32	Jones Park	Lakeview @ Timberland Drive
38	Pace/Tim's Funeral home	Leach St
39	New Addition/ North Lufkin	Wilson St, Kelty's St
44	Charlie Malone's Horeshoe Motel	Walker Quarters
45	Parilee Dodd barbershop	Kelty's St
60	Stephano Joseph & Son Grocery	324 N. Angelina Ave.
61	Dance Hall	Walker Quarters
63	East Tex. Cotton Club	Wilson & Culverhouse
66	Congo Club	Directly behind Walker Quarters
69	Brandon School	Keltys Drive
70	Greater Shiloh Baptist	1519 Williams St @ Hosea Dolphus Sr.Ave
71	Little Ducks End	Owned by Clyde Davis in Walkers Quarters
72	New Zion Church (Original)	North Raquet passed Abney
75	Pace Funeral Home, E.Tx. Undertaking	218 Leach St @ Lakeview

77	Horseshoe Motel	Owned by Charlie Malone near Wilson St in New Addition
81	Station One Post Office	Operated by S.T. Lewis in North Lufkin
82	Dr. S.C. Packard's clinic	On now MLK
83	Angelina Lumber	Keltys section bounded by N. Raquet St, Kurth Dr north of Abney St.
88	Geneva's Drive-In	620 Kurth Drive
93	Garrett Elementary School Original Dunbar High	Current site, Leacher St & Kurth Dr.
94	Lincoln Theatre owned by Joe Stefano	Keltys St, where Congo Club was located

Table 5. Site Locations for North Addition

Original Map using approximate site locations referenced by contemporary inhabitants

13
Cotton Club

Clemmie T. and Willie Parker owned the Cotton Club. The Club was named after the famous nightclub in New York City that operated during and after Prohibition. It was possible that Dr. Claude Stewart, the only black doctor in Lufkin, was also a part-owner of the East Texas Cotton Club. The Club operated from the early 1940s to the 1960s. After World War II, teachers ran a trade school at the club for returning veterans. S.T. Lewis ran a taxi service from the club.[103]

Fig. 133. Square Deal Taxi Stand, c.1956.
"The Mirror 1955-56," Negro Chamber of Commerce and Dunbar High School

The Boosters Club was a group of men that worked for the Southern Pacific Railroad, which ran from Houston to Shreveport. These men were brakemen and their wives organized themselves and would do things like fashion shows and dances. The wives were members of the Brakemen's Wives Club and they liked to host dances and banquets at the Cotton Club. These women were best dressed with diamond rings and beautiful earrings. They would be an active part of the community in bringing activities there. Women met there for social clubs, hosting fashion shows and other programs. But it was the entertainment that made the club famous. [104]

The East Texas Cotton Club started as a small store. It later expanded into a dance hall that also functioned as a social center. This club was part of the 'Chitlin Circuit.' Since blacks performing in white clubs were restricted or forbidden, they had to play in auditoriums, roadshows, or black clubs across the country, in venues called the 'Chitlin Circuit.'

The name of this uniquely African American itinerary undoubtedly was chosen in honor of the cooked hog intestines called 'chitlings' that were a stable in most Negro kitchens at the time. *"Anybody that was somebody played there. It was one of the elite clubs in our city and they would bring in performers. Lufkin got these acts because they were being booked in white clubs and were limited by the few Negro clubs who had the financial ability to pay them.* **Kennedy**[105]

The Cotton Club was located at the intersection of Wilson Street and Culverhouse. It provided musical entertainment and positively impacted the relationship between the black and white in the community because of its diverse customer base. *"Integration [in Lufkin] started there because the white kids wanted to come and hear these outstanding entertainers."*[106] It was a BYOB (bring your own booze) club restricted to adults. Popular dance steps at the time included "Swing Out" and "Slow Drag"[107] Those who lived in Nacogdoches and wanted to go to the club had to board buses to travel to the Lufkin dance hall. Zoot suits were trendy attire for the young African American and Hispanic men and a perfect look for the club scene.

Zoot suits had a distinctive design where the coat came down near the knees. The pants had wide knees and narrow bottoms called drapes. The oversized vest that came up almost to your chin was long.

Zoot suits were frowned upon in Nacogdoches, so the men would wear street clothes, hide their suits in a bag to board the buses and then change when they arrived in Lufkin.[108]

Fig. 134. Dancing in a Zoot Suit, c. 1944.
The Journal of Dress, Body & Culture, 2004

This suit was so controversial in some areas of the country that negative sentiment led to the so-called Los Angeles Zoot Suit Riots. Gangs of Navy seamen would stream into the City of Los Angeles. They would pull suit wearers (primarily Hispanic) from buildings or off the streets, beat them and often strip them of the offending garb.[109]

Women wore their hair in a 'pompadour.' The hairstyle made famous by many celebrities swept the hair straight up from the forehead into a high, turned-back roll. The women wore long, full skirts that ran past their knees. The length made them very suitable for the high-energy dance steps of the time, such as the "Jitterbug" and the "Chicken." The men also sported the same pompadour hairstyle. Dances events were a frequent event at the Club. They were held at least once a week. The biggest crowds ranged from 200 to 300 patrons. [110]

Black performers en route to show dates in large cities stopped in Lufkin because they knew the club would draw crowds. Entertainers included:

Fig. 135. Ray Charles Fig. 136. Little Richard

Wikipedia Commons
Ray Charles: Grammy Winner, Hall of Fame

Arts and Culture Lifestyle News, May 2020
Grammy Winner, Hall of Fame

Fig. 137. B.B. King
Wikipedia Commons
B.B. King: Grammy, Hall of Fame
When B.B. King came to play in Lufkin, he would call all the children in the neighborhood up and buy them chips at the concession stand and then let them touch his guitars. "[111]

Fig. 138. Duke Ellington
Biography.com
Duke Ellington: Grammy, Hall of Fame

Fig. 139. Fats Domino
Wikipedia Commons
Fats Domino: Grammy Winner, Hall of Fame

Fig. 140. T. Bone Walker
Wikipedia.org
T-Bone Walker: Grammy Winner
T-Bone Walker. [112] *An American blues guitarist, singer, songwriter, and multi-instrumentalist was a pioneer and innovator of jump blues and electric blues sound.*

Fig. 141. Sammy Davis Jr.   Fig. 142. Ike and Tina Turner

Wikipedia Commons
Grammy winners
Hall of Fame

Other notable performers included:
Joe Turner - Barron of the Boogie
The Daughters of Rhythm and the Sweethearts of Rhythm
Ivory Joe Hunter.
Junior Walker and the All-Stars

Fig. 143. Ethel Waters, c.1943
Gospel Hall of Fame   Grammy Hall of Fame

Fig. 144. Otis Redding
Wikipedia Commons
Grammy award winner
Hall of Fame

The Cotton Club closed around 1967. The building was later torn down in the 1990s. What remains are the memories of *"the fashions, the dances, the songs, the cafes, the entertainers that worked there and what this building meant to the community of north Lufkin." "It really was the hub of this area."*[113] Kennedy

Although the Cotton Club was the most famous entertainment center, it certainly wasn't the only club in Lufkin. The city was dotted with dance clubs and domino shacks throughout the black community. Clyde Davis had two little nightclub dance halls. One of them was near the trestles off of Cotton Belt. He also owned the Little Ducks End in Walker's Quarters. McClendon (unconfirmed if this was Dr. Charles McClendon) had a big dance club on Wilson Street. House of Blue Lights near Lufkin Land was also a dance club. Pine Grove Hall on Grove Street was another club built by the Parker brothers.

Another combination dance club and hotel was called the Paradise Inn. Negroes enjoyed music, dance and generally appreciated each other's company. *"During those brief moments of fun and enjoyment, the average Negro didn't feel the segregation and discrimination. It was just having fun."*[114]

14
Hallowed Ground

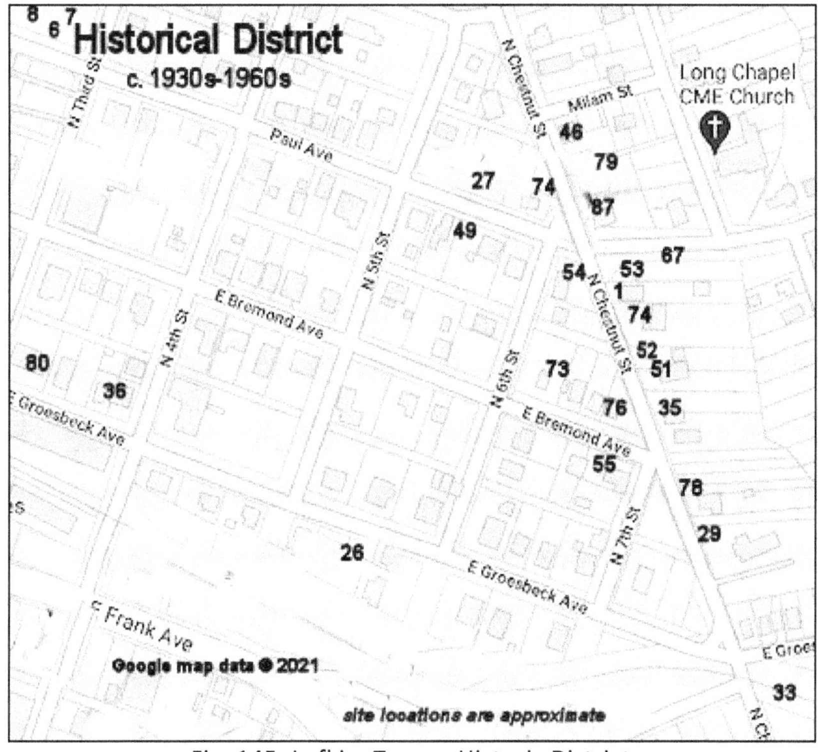

Fig. 145. Lufkin, Texas - Historic District
Google (2021) map data
Original Map using approximate site locations referenced by contemporary inhabitants

The single-floor, framed building with two street addresses located at 428/430 Chestnut was Montana Lillie and his daughter's homes. Some called this area known as the Historic District "Hallowed Ground." It was probably built by Reverend Betty Kennedy's father, Will Ingram, with help from his crew, including Montana Lille. Reverend Kennedy called this area "Hallowed Ground" during Vera Price's (the author's mother) eulogy. It was the site of Lucky Ward Colored School before Montana bought it. Before Montana purchased this property in 1936, it was rumored to have had a bright and colorful history. Besides being Lufkin's first high school for Negroes, it also hosted at various times a barbershop, rent houses, supper club with dancing, a church and a café. The two "shotgun" houses that Montana built in the back of the property was also said to be at one time a doctor's office, a hospital and a dentist's office at one time before.

However, its rich and historical significance was secondary for those who called this location home. This location was a solid wooden structure with outdated wiring. Open bulbs hung in some rooms for light. The house was sturdy, thanks to the passage of time that almost petrified the wood. It was jokingly speculated that it was doubtful this house could ever burn. Unfortunately, the house was built near a creek which contributed to the ever-present sound of rats scurrying in the attic and the uninsulated walls. Fortunately, they only occasionally decided to share a bed with its occupants.

Fig. 146. Montana Lillie Home, c. 2006
(Author's family photograph)
Montana Lillie home at 430 N. Chestnut St.
Formerly Lucky Ward High School

Ownership of the land can be traced as far back as 1716 when the Spanish Crown distributed land grants.

428/430 Chestnut Deed – property changing ownership

1716	Land grants made by Spanish crown to establish mission and presidio in East Texas (21)	
1820	Spanish government passed law to open Texas foreigners (90)	Voided when Mexico won their Independence from Spain
1829	Lorenzo DeZavala granted empresio to settle 500 families in East Texas (22)	Along Sabine river from Nacogdoches to Gulf of Mexico, 50 miles wide
1830	DeZavala sold his land to the Galveston Bay & Texas Land Co. (90)	This was illegal. Land wasn't settled
1835	John L Quinalty purchased 4 leagues (Sabine empresio) (91)	
1858	Henry Raquet bought from Quinalty 1 league	Including the property that would become Montana's
1861	Raquet estate sold to George Cook	Cook died without a will. Sold for $1.50 an acre
1869	Cook estate sold to H.G. Lane	
1895	JH Chapman bought land	
1903	Chapman sold to Trustees of Colored School District no. 2 (2 lots)	Land purchased for the Lucky Ward Colored School. $75 down, $62.50/mo. for 24 months
1929	Lufkin ISD sold to Dr. D.S. Simmons	Lufkin ISD had taken over by this time
193x	Dr. Simmons sold to Angelina Lodge no. 5268 Grand Order of Fellows	
1936	**Montana Lilly bought land**	**Sold for $1008, $50 down & 47 installments of $20/month**
2011	Lilly estate sold to Vera Price	
2014	Vera Price estate sold to Jackson	

Table 6. Title History for 428_429 Deed

[115]20, [116]21, [117]22, [118]90, [119]91

Note: 428/430 Chestnut, Chapman addition lots 3 and 4 ownership history

Source: Montana Lillie Deed title search (1858-1936)

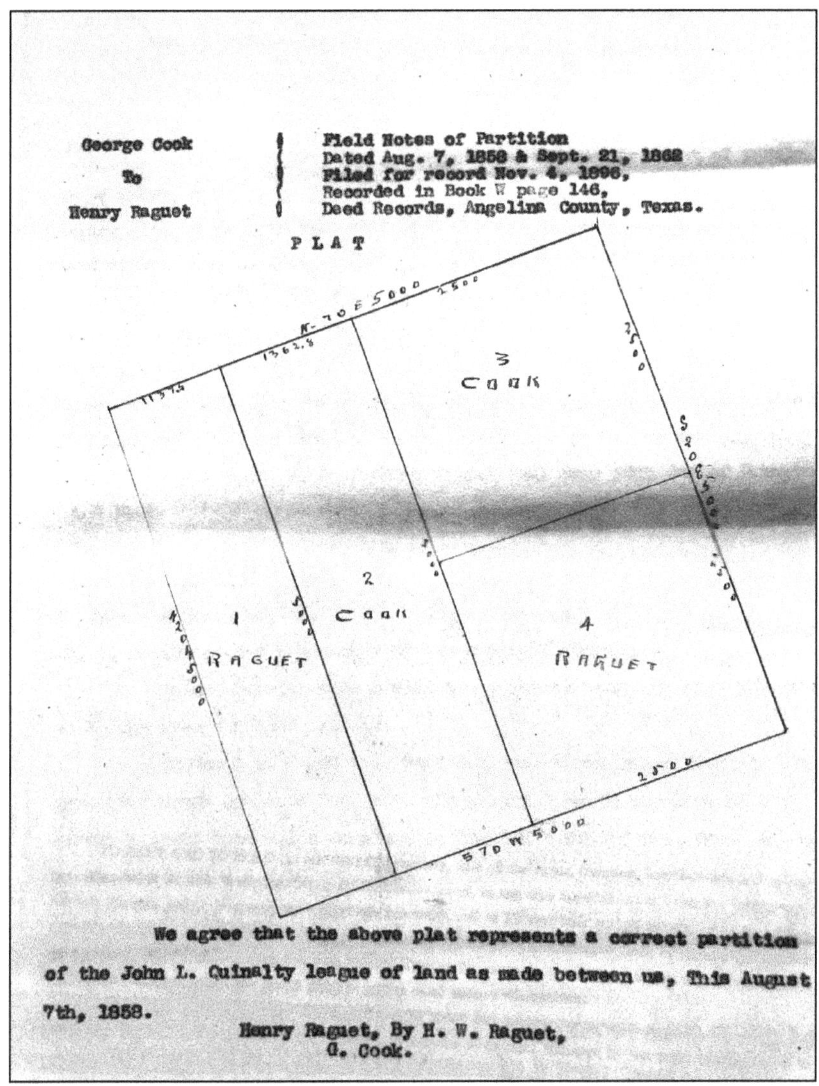

Fig. 147. Lucky Ward Deeded Plat

(Author's family photograph)
428/430 Chestnut Deeded Plat
John L. Quinalty League of Land, c. 1858 [120]

Fig. 148. Typical Country Outhouse of the Period
Free Stock Photos. Stockvault.net

Much like many Negro homes of the time, this homestead on Chestnut originally had no indoor plumbing. The floors were wooden pine. A double-sided outhouse provided toilet facilities in the backyard shared by families in two homes and two rental houses. Alternatively, there was a "slop bucket" inside each home for the nighttime that had to be emptied regularly. Of course, the children assumed the undesirable responsibility of taking the bucket outside to empty in the outhouse.

Fig. 149. Galvanized Metal Washtub
Worthpoint.com
(Also known as a #3 washtub.)

The lack of indoor plumbing (except for running water) forced everyone to bathe in steel, round washtubs. Water was heated and poured into the tubs. It was required to mix the various hot and cold temperatures to ensure its effectiveness to clean without scalding. These tubs were also used to wash clothes and do other everyday household chores. They were cheap and indestructible, ensuring their prominent position in any poor person's home. They were small enough for children to wash but not much larger than that.

The same washtub was also filled with warm hog intestines secured from fresh hogs at the slaughterhouse less than a mile away on Chestnut. On warm, breezy days, there was no doubt that the business of killing hogs could be smelled in the air in the immediate area.

15
Montana Folklore

Fig. 150. 428/430 Chestnut, c. 1970
(Family home, c. 1936 – c. 2011)

In the backyard of 428/430 N. Chestnut, Montana owned a falling down storage building containing his tools of the trade (e.g., hammers, saws, nails, etc.). Next to the building was a huge pile of wood representing scrap from various projects. The woodpile was put to regular use by the children who felt the desire to construct their personal projects, such as wooden models of tanks, trucks, ramps, missile launchers, shields, etc. Perhaps a more purposeful use of the wood as kindling to fire one of Emma's two large cast-iron kettle pots. She made her own disinfectant soap and clothes cleaner called lye soap. Using the same techniques employed by her slave ancestors, Emma made this soap by boiling lard, lye and water. The resultant liquidly mass was allowed to dry and harden before being cut into sections and used as needed.

Fig. 151. One Mule and the Land
Library of Congress

Fig. 152. Doing Laundry with a Scrub Board & Tub
Library of Congress, Washington, D.C.

To call lye soap "harsh" is like saying a root canal causes some discomfort. However, Emma would first boil the clothes clean in an outdoor cast-iron kettle with this cheap but powerful cleaner. She would then wash the clothes in a washtub to remove any remnants of the soap. After the wash, Emma would run them through a manual ringer that squeezed much of the water from the clothes. Finally, she would hang them outside to dry in the sun and wind on clotheslines secured with clothespins.

Emma raised chicken that provided a source of fresh eggs and eventually fresh meat. The natural yellow skin of the poultry resulting from feeding them so much corn was an unappreciated delicacy.

Montana contributed mightily to this necessity of self-sufficiency. He plowed roughly a one-acre plot behind the house using trusty mules and plowshares every year.

He fertilized the property with cow manure from friends and neighbors because he didn't own any livestock. Despite his almost archaic farming methods, Montana rarely failed to grow beautiful corn, tomatoes, collard greens, cabbage and other vegetables to supplement the hunting, fishing and chickens. He had two pear trees, a fig tree and a cherry tree on this same plot as an added treat. Consequently, there was a constant battle with the numerous birds and wildlife for their fruit.

Montana struck the classic rugged pose that Hollywood would appreciate. He stood 6-foot, 3-inches tall, typically dressed in long johns, long-sleeved, buttoned-down khaki shirts and khaki slacks even in the dead of the East Texas summer heat and work boots. Even a casual glance at this human being and one would leave with the clear understanding that he was a no-nonsense man.

Whether or not he was actually called "Mountain Man" or even if the term was used in talking about him cannot be confirmed. However, if the term wasn't used in reference to him, it should have been. He would have worn the moniker well. It was amazing how he endured so many challenges; due to many indignities, so many things that would challenge the very soul of one's spirit. Yet, through it all, he remained proud, confident and spirited. The eerily contrast to this rugged pose he struck were his eyes. They were rainbow-colored – gray, hazel and blue or brown. The grandchildren always surmised that he must have had white or Indian blood. Given his curious eye color led them to their less than worldly conclusion.

Montana was only one generation removed from his bloodline who was in firm control of a Louisiana plantation slaveholder. Many years later, DNA testing by his descendants indicated he probably had Irish and or British lineage. Little did the grandchildren realize that they were probably correct.

He was a man who had to work with his hands. It didn't matter whether it was his many jobs in the sawmills, later as a carpenter or just building his home on Chestnut. He kept busy. It was somewhat of side entertainment to see him try to sit still. His hands and feet were always in perpetual motion – hammering that imaginary nail, moving that log from times past, something, anything.

Let it not be said that Montana struggled to find times to relax. However, watching and following the local Paul Lawrence Dunbar football team play was a noticeable exception. He would attend the local games with his son-in-law Clark and the family. He would follow the Fighting Tigers on the road during the Negro Texas High School playoffs when the opportunity allowed.

During another of those rare moments when the work, sweat-stained hat came off, he did enjoy recalling a good story from his incredible past. Children would roll their eyes and giggle in disbelief, not knowing that there was a lot of truth embedded in these fantastic stories of struggle, triumph, and challenge. He could tell it so well because he lived it. Yes, the passage of time might have provided him the opportunity to embellish or "misremember" specific facts. Make no mistake about it. His grandchildren should have paid closer attention and better appreciated the legacy that Montana was leaving because it would endure for future generations.

Occasionally, during those moments of relaxation, Montana would find his way into the kitchen. This was not a room that he frequented a lot.

On the other hand, Emma was locally renowned for her culinary skills. She could bake, boil and fry expertly. Emma was a proud member of probably the last generation of American women who knew how to churn butter, make buttermilk and biscuits from scratch. Emma cooked with lard, butter, buttermilk and things grown or killed recently. Before Emma could prepare the delicious meals in her old kitchen with an ancient stove, dented cookware and limited devices, she would often go into the family garden.

Fig. 153. Churning Butter
EncyclopediaofAlabama.org

Here Emma could pick (depending on the season) corn, cabbage, collards, tomatoes, cucumbers and all manner of deliciousness. All these wonderful foodstuffs represented the fruits of labor from Montana's one-acre plot of land that he tilled with mule and plow and was tended by the entire family, including Emma and the grandchildren.

Emma churned her butter, made soap, made her own clothes, and preserved fruits and vegetables. She made scratch biscuits and raised her chickens for meat and eggs. Emma could hunt and fish and dipped snuff continuously. She could hand stitch an intricate quilt with a century-old manual sowing machine.

Emma did all these wearing ankle-length dresses and an ever-present apron. Not once in her life does anyone remember her showing so much as her ankles. Not once. In short, she was one of the most self-sufficient women of the last generation of independent women and the perfect mate for Montana Lillie. She was every bit his match. She had a small, limited freezer that was unnecessary and didn't work too well. Of course, this required cooking two to three meals every day. The concept of leftovers was limited. Not only because Emma and Montana preferred their food fresh but also because she lived next to her daughter Vera, who raised a girl, three growing, active boys who knew that a good meal was available for a limited time from "Big Mamma." The lone exception was during the holidays when Emma would bake probably six to eight cakes and pies and put them in her dining room. This annual event triggered four to six weeks of continuous availability of desserts of all types.

Montana's favorite foods began and ended with pinto beans, rice and cornbread. He could and often would eat this combination six days a week. This steadfast preference left Emma the flexibility to vary the Sunday meal after church. When Montana stepped into the kitchen, it was not so ambitious. He claimed his pinto beans were "world-famous." When Montana got into the kitchen, it was as if the world stopped and paid close attention. The meal he produced was relatively unremarkable.   However, the children and grandchildren didn't seem to matter. It was the culmination of a life play that wasn't repeated that frequently.

One of his fantastic beliefs was that the car radio in his black Studebaker could pick up the broadcast from China! It was true that when the car was parked in the drive and the children were allowed to put his claim to the test; they heard a strange and foreign language being spoken.

The younger children were wowed at such prowess. There was some skepticism of the claim, given that we were told that China was literally on the other side of the world. The unsuspecting children were told that it was possible to find special caverns and crevices, fall through and come out on the other side of the world in China! The broadcast was all talking and no music. Later the children came to appreciate that, given the proximity to the Mexican radio stations in Houston that the broadcast was probably in Spanish. At that time, Lufkin had almost no Hispanics living in town. There were no Spanish-language channels available on television. So the lack of exposure to languages other than American and East Texan (yes, these are two separate languages) was somewhat excusable.

The Studebaker was central to the Lillie household. Not only did it serve as Montana's escape pod, but it was used on the 3rd Sunday of every month to take him, Emma and Vera's eldest daughter, to "dinner on the ground," a church-sponsored picnic back in Many, Louisiana. They were greeted in the morning by Emma's parents, Melissa "Maw Maw" Hill and William "Bill" Hill. Melissa would have prepared a great breakfast of country ham, bacon, biscuits and fresh hen eggs. Hours later, after church, they would join the congregation in another large meal. Just to ensure everyone went home fed, Melissa would offer another big meal before the trip back to Lufkin. This generosity made finishing each meal an ordeal. Melissa was not a person to disappoint. Although standing a mere 4-foot, 11-inches tall, she would curse incessantly, including in the presence of her 6-foot, 4-inch husband, Bill.

Unfortunately, the Studebaker once plowed into a deer that appeared to come out of nowhere on one faithful trip to Many.

The collision resulted in another dinner table meal and a crushed front end to the beloved Studebaker. Montana strapped some rope around the hood and car frame to keep the hood closed in typical Montana fashion. This temporary fix remained in place for the life of the vehicle.[121]

Speaking of the Studebaker, when Montana and Emma often had some disagreement, he would hop into his personal rocket ship and "burn rubber" all the way to the stop sign at Chestnut and Paul Ave, one block away.

There were two long, vintage shotguns of at least four or five feet in length stored in the closet in his house. Because Montana was an avid hunter for food, he kept a bag of shells in the closet. He frequently traveled back to his favorite lands in Louisiana to hunt deer, rabbits, squirrels, raccoons and just about anything else that dared to rear its head. Between Montana's game hunting and Emma's fishing, the dinner table in Lufkin was filled with food procured by their own hands and not bought in a grocery store. This abundance of food explains why the family who lacked so much financially enjoyed great meals.

There is a story of when the children almost lost their hearing by exploding shells between two bricks. The fascination with the pellets and shot when a shotgun shell is disassembled got the better of them. The resulting explosive sound of the shot greatly exceeded cap guns.

The idiotic and juvenile practice of sneaking out a couple of shells occasionally so as not to be missed was suddenly halted for all time one faithful morning after the unauthorized firing.

The shells were confiscated and disassembled by the young thief. The shot was readied. The sound from the resulting explosion was trapped by surrounding walls and not allowed to dissipate. The sound was so loud that it left a ringing in the ear of the perpetrator (the author) and caused a temporary loss of hearing. Unfortunately, the children didn't fully appreciate the difference between exploding a shell in the wide open or doing it near Montana's porch surrounded by solid walls.

The perpetrator was terrified at what he had done to himself but was too afraid to seek help. The threat of a whipping exceeded the desire to seek medical attention. Fortunately for the temporarily deaf grandchild, the deafness dissipated and the hearing returned in a few hours.

Fig. 154. 1956 Studebaker
Smartmotorguide.com
Similar to what Montana owned but a LOT nicer

Also, in the closet with the shotgun, Montana owned a blue and white striped seersucker jacket. No one ever saw him wear it, but its very appearance silently spoke of another day and time when the burden of family or the excesses of youth permitted this Mountain Man to wear such a pretty thing. Next to that odd jacket was his black suit—the one he wore every Sunday when Emma and Montana attended New Zion Baptist Church. Come Sunday, Montana would put on his black suit, hair slicked down with country pomade, clean shirt and a wide brim hat tilted just slightly off-center and head off to services at the same church he built by hand.

Last Days

Per his death certificate, Montana died of uremia due to chronic inflammation. He had been transported from his home on Chestnut (for 50 years) to Rusk State Hospital in Rusk, Texas. Within two weeks, Montana McKinney Lillie was dead.

The fact that this proud independent man ended up at such an early age of 71, sick and unaware, is the ultimate irony and sadness. He had progressive kidney failure that might have been treated if he had been provided access to the most modern medical facilities of his time. The kidney failure allowed a buildup of urea in his blood, leading to dementia.

Fig. 155. Montana Lillie Grave Site

Fig. 156. Emma Lillie Grave Site
(Author's personal photographs)

"The beauty of the soul shines out when a man bears with composure one heavy mischance after another, not because he does not feel them, but because he is a man of high and heroic temper." Aristotle

Fig. 157. The White Dove as a Messenger of the Dead
Not Out. 67notout.com

"We have come through times of shame and mistreatment and abuse of our people, yet we have stood and we have risen to such high heights that we have been able to see our children and grandchildren achieve goals that were not open to us and yet we fight each day for a better tomorrow for those of our people. I think preserving our people in a living history certainly is going to help to better our hope." **Kennedy**

Appendix 1 – Family Tree

By the time Montana was born, he had already been preceded by 13 siblings. Little did he know that two additional sisters would follow him in birth. His father, Allen and mother, Georgia, would ultimately have 16 children. Montana was one of 8 boys. Georgia would give birth to all 16 children over 23 years.

Montana and Emma had three children – Berta Mae, born 1920; L.C., born 1922 and Vera, born 1926.
Montana died on January 15, 1972 (almost 71 years to the day).

Fig. 158. Emma Lillie, c. 1950s
(Author's family photograph)
Montana's Wife
Emma Lillie, around age 50

Montana's wife Emma was born July 3, 1903, in Many, Louisiana. She was one of seven siblings. Although all seven children were born in Louisiana, only John, the eldest child and Huston died in their native state. The four daughters of William and Melissa – all lived long lives averaging over 95.

Fig. 159. Bobby Jindal
Wikipedia Commons
Montana's sister, Leola, was honored by the Gov. of Louisiana, Jindal, as the oldest living Louisianan. She lived to 104.

Fig. 160. L.C. Lillie, c. 1970s.
(Author's family photograph)
LC Lillie, about age 45 – son
Montana's Son
Owner of the Blue Room on N. Chestnut St

Fig. 161. Patricia Lillie McKenzie, c. 1960s
(Author's family photograph)
Patricia McKenzie, about age 20
Montana's Niece
Noted Lufkin History Maker

Fig. 162. Clark Jackson Price, c. 1948.
(Author's family photographs)
Son-in-Law of Montana Lillie and Texas Foundry Employee

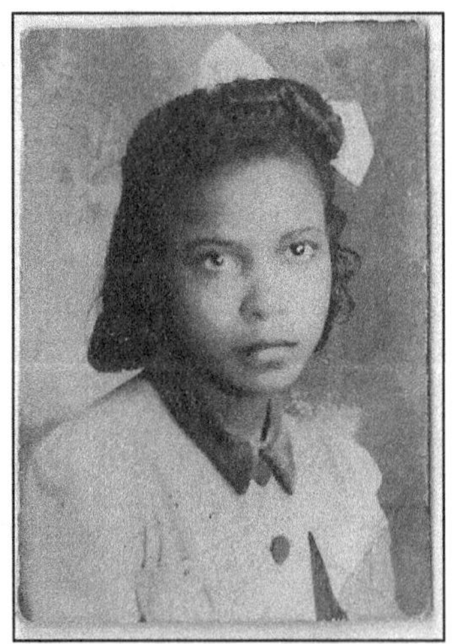

Fig. 163. Vera Lillie Price, c. 1940s.
(Author's family photographs)
*Vera Lillie Price, at age 20 around when she was married to Clark
19 years old
Montana's Daughter*

Appendix 2 – Texas History

The title search completed to purchase Lots 3 and 4 of the Chapman Addition from the Quintalty League reflects a significant peek into Texas land ownership history. This search traces the property ownership from the 18th century under Spanish rule through the historic purchase of the same land for the Lucky Ward School. The terms and people referenced in the title search could be foreign to the modern reader.

Land Grants[122]

The history of land grants in Texas is long. The Spanish Crown made the earliest grant to establish a mission and presidio in East Texas in 1716.

In Nacogdoches and other areas along the northern frontier, families usually received land through oral agreements with local officials. With the beginning of the American incursion into the Nacogdoches area in the 1790s, many families sought to formalize these grants to preserve their rights. Despite granting large tracts of land in the north, the number of inhabitants of the region remained small. Spanish officials experimented with a policy to entice settlers from the American frontier with promises of land, religious tolerance, and special privileges to populate the area. In 1820 the Spanish government passed a measure to open Texas to foreigners who would respect the laws and constitution of Spain.

This act was replaced by the Homestead Act of 1854, which reduced homestead grants to 160 acres and required three years' residence. The policy of homestead grants was continued under acts of 1866 and 1870 and under the Constitution of 1876. The amount of land disposed of under Texas's pre-emption and homestead laws are recorded at 4,847,136 acres.

However, the most controversial of the empresario grants were David G. Burnet, Joseph Vehlein, and Lorenzo de Zavala. They sold their respective contracts to New York and Boston speculators. In October 1830, Burnet negotiated the sale of his grant to the Galveston Bay and Texas Land Company, as did Vehlein's agent. The sale was Lorenzo de Zavala, a native of Yucatán, a prominent politician and currently a political refugee in New York City. He had acquired the long fifty-two-mile-wide border reserve on the Sabine River as his empresario grant in 1828 when he agreed to settle 500 European or Mexican families. He, too, never saw his Texas land nor sent a colonist.

Fig. 164. Lorenzo de Zavala
Handbook of Texas Online
Lorenzo de Zavala, former Republic of Texas Vice President[123]

Empresarios

Empresarios did not own the land within their grants, nor could they issue titles; the state-appointed a land commissioner to give deeds only after 100 families had been settled. Surveyors laid off leagues and laborers along the watercourses and roads, after which colonists could choose vacant tracts. The settlers paid fees to the state, the surveyor, the land commissioner, and the clerk, who wrote the deeds on stamped paper and recorded the payments.

MEXICAN AND SPANISH TITLES. 651

NAME OF GRANTEE.	WHEN ISSUED.	QUANTITY.	WHERE SITUATED.
Power & Hewitson	Nov'r 29, '3	11 leagues	San Patricio.
Padro, Francisco, (see Power & Hewitson)			
Padro, Jose Anselmo	Oct'r 17, '34	1 league	Angelina.
Padro, Jose Martin	May 18, '26	1 league	Trinity, Houston.
Padro, Juan	Dec'r 4, "	1-3 league	Jefferson or Liberty.
Prater, William	July 19, '24	1 lea 1 lab	lea Brazoria, lab Austin.
Prather, Stephen	Nov'r 25, '35	10 leagues	?
Prentiss, Henry B.	April 20 '33	1 league	Harris.
Prewitt, Beasley	May 2, '31		Lot in town of Liberty.
Prewitt, Beasley	April 23, "	1 league	Liberty.
Prewitt, Cinda Riley	May 2, "		Lot in town of Liberty.
Prewitt, Jacob	Feb'y 16, '35	1 league	Houston.
Price, G. W.	July 10, "	1-4 league	Freestone.
Price, James	Feb'y 22, '3:	1 league	Washington.
Prickett, Jacob	Jan'y 21, '35	1-4 league	Robertson.
Priestly, Philander	De'r 10, '3:	1-4 league	Gonzales.
Prince, R.	Sep'r 30, '35	1 league	Tyler.
Prior, Mary	Dec'r 20, '3:	1 league	Falls.
Prissick, William	June 15, '35	1 league	Houston.
Pritchard, Joseph	" 21, "	1-4 league	Houston, ?
Procela, Jose de Jesus	July 22, "	1 league	Houston.
Procela, Jose Maria	" 17, "	1 league	Smith, Cherokee.
Procela, Jose Maria, by M. Murcheson, att'y	Feb'y 7, '3:	1 league	Houston.
Procela, Jose Policarpio	Oct'r 12, '35	1 league	"
Procela, Manuel	Nov'r 13, "	1 league	Tyler, Jefferson.
Procela, Pedro	May 8, '16	?	Nacogdoches.
Prm. Maria Josefa	Aug't 26, '35	1 league	Rusk.
Pruitt, John	July 9, "	1 league	Tyler, ?
Pruitt, Pleasant	" 24, '24	1 league	Matagorda.
Pry, Peter B.	Nov'r 7, '3:	1 league	Jasper.
Pryor, William	Aug't 24, '2:	1 labor	Austin.
Pryor, William	May 21, '2:	1 league	Washington.
Pugh, Spencer A.	May 6, '3:	1 league	Fayette.
Punchard, William	Sep'r 11, '35	1 league	Milam.
Punchard, Joseph, heirs of	July 6, "	24 labors	Hill.
Purdom, Henry	Sep'r 17, "	24 labors	Bell, Milam.
Purdom, Henry	March 18, "	1 league	Falls.
Purdy, Letson	Dec'r 30, '3:	1 league	Robertson.
Quevedo, Thomas	Sep'r 23, '35	11 leagues	1 Ange'a, 7 Smith, 3 Ch'kee.
Quinalty, John L.	Nov'r 10, "	1-4 league	Sabine.
Quinalty, Joseph Lewis	April 27, "	1 league	Angelina.
Quinn, Bridget	Oct'r 12, '3:	1 league	San Patricio.
Quinn, James	April 23, '25		Lot in town of Victoria.
Quinn, William	Dec'r 12, '3:	1 league	San Patricio.
Quinn, William	Nov'r 22, "	1-4 league	" "
Quinn, William & Patrick	" 20, "	1 2 league	" "
Quirk, Edmund	Feb'y 19, '06	4 leagues	San Augustine.
Quirk, Edmund & Michael	Oct'r 30, '3:	1-4 league	Goliad.
Quirk, Thomas	Dec'r 25, "	1-4 league	Goliad, Refugio.
Rabago, Miguel, by S. M. Williams, att'y	Jan'y 13, "	11 leagues	McLennan.
Rabb, Andrew	Aug't 10, '2:	1 1-2 league	Wharton.
Rabb, John	July 8, "	1 lea 2 labs	lea Ft. Bend, labs Austin.
Rabb, Thomas J.	" 24, "	1 league	Wharton.
Rabb, William	" 19, "	5 leagues	3 Fayette, 2 Matagorda.

League[125]

A "league" can also be a unit of area used to express the land area equal to 25 million square yards. A (square) league is equivalent to about 4,428.4 acres. (It was used in the archaic system of old Spanish land grants affecting Texas and parts of adjoining states. This use of league is used throughout the Texas Constitution.

Fig. 165. Major Henry Wynkoop Raquet
Southern Methodist University Library

RAGUET, HENRY WYNKOOP (1824–1862). Henry Wynkoop Raguet, merchant and Confederate officer, was born in Cincinnati, Hamilton County, Ohio, on June 29, 1824, to Henry and Marcia Anne (Towers) Raguet. The elder Henry Raguet, a veteran of the War of 1812, traveled to New Orleans in 1832 following the collapse of his mercantile business. He met Sam Houston, who encouraged him to settle in the Nacogdoches area of East Texas.[126]

Notes

[1] Wikipedia contributors. "Natchitoches, Louisiana." Wikipedia, The Free Encyclopedia. Wikipedia, The Free Encyclopedia, 6 Aug. 2021. Web. 16 Aug. 2021.

[2] Green, James R. "The Brotherhood of Timber Workers 1910-1913: A Radical Response to Industrial Capitalism in the Southern USA." The Past and Present Society. Oxford University Press. No. 6 (August 1973). pp. 161-200.

[3] Fricker, Donna. "The Louisiana Lumber Boom, c.1880-1925", Historic Preservation Services LLC. National Archives and Records Great Lakes Region (Chicago). Published 1970. pg. 27.

[4] Stokes, George Alvin. "A Study of the Industry As a Culturo-Geographic Factor Lumbering in Southwest Louisiana." A Dissertation. Louisiana State University, May 1954, pg. 26.

[5] Green, James R. "The Brotherhood of Timber Workers 1910-1913: A Radical Response to Industrial Capitalism in the Southern USA." The Past and Present Society. Oxford University Press. No. 6 (August 1973). pp. 161-200.

[6] ibid.

[7] Payne, Charles, Green, Adam, editors. Time Longer Than Rope.

[8] Boon, Effie Mattox. "History of Angelina County." Ancestry.com. M.A. Thesis, University of Texas. Austin, Texas. August 1937.

[9] Haltom, R.W. "History and Description of Angelina County, Texas." The Pemperton Press, Jenkins Publishing Company. Austin, New York. October 1888

[10] Bowman, Bob Editor. "You'll Love Lufkin." City of Lufkin.com, cityoflufkin.com/history.htm. Accessed 11 July 2010.

[11] ibid.

[12] ibid., (63) Bowman, Bob & Doris. "The Forgotten Towns of East Texas.", Best of East Texas Publishers. Vol. 1.

[13] ibid.

[14] ibid.

[15] Biesele, Megan. "Angelina County." Handbook of Texas Online, Accessed 2 June 2020, tshaonline.org/handbook/entries/angelina. Published by the Texas State Historical Association

[16] Wooster, Ralph A. "Life in Civil War East Texas." East Texas Historical Society Journal. Vol. III, no. 3, October 1965, pg. 93

[17] Bowman, Bob Editor. "You'll Love Lufkin." City of Lufkin.com, cityoflufkin.com/history.htm. Accessed 11 July 2010.

18 Biesele, Megan. "Angelina County." Handbook of Texas Online, Accessed 2 June 2020, tshaonline.org/handbook/entries/angelina. Published by the Texas State Historical Association

19 History Book Committee of Lufkin Geological Society Editors, Lufkin, Texas. History of Angelina County (1846-1991). Curtis Media Corporation, Dallas, Texas.

20 Kennedy, Betty. Interview 170b. By R.L Kuykendall. 12 Sep. 2002. Diboll History Center.

21 ibid.

22 ibid.

23 ibid.

24 ibid.

25 Kennedy, Betty. Interview 170a. By R.L Kuykendall. 12 Sep. 2002. Diboll History Center.

26 Rhodes, Odis O. Interview 232b. By R.L Kuykendall. 2001. Diboll History Center.

27 ibid.

28 Carrington, Sr. Ellis. Interview 244a. By R.L Kuykendall. 15 and 29 Jul 2002. Diboll History Center.

29 Rhodes, Odis O. Interview 232b. By R.L Kuykendall. 2001. Diboll History Center.

30 ibid.

31 "History – Brown v. Board of Education". United States Courts. uscourts.gov/educational-resources. Accessed 15 Dec 2018.

32 Rhodes, Odis O. Interview 232b. By R.L Kuykendall. 2001. Diboll History Center.

33 ibid.

34 Rhodes, Odis O. Interview 232a. By R.L Kuykendall. 10Jan 2001. Diboll History Center.

35 Carrington, Sr. Ellis. Interview 244a. By R.L Kuykendall. 15 and 29 Jul 2002. Diboll History Center

36 ibid.

37 Carrington, Sr. Ellis. Interview 244a. By R.L Kuykendall. 15 and 29 Jul 2002. Diboll History Center

38 Boon, Effie Mattox. "History of Angelina County." Ancestry.com. M.A. Thesis, University of Texas. Austin, Texas. August 1937.

39 Boon, Effie Mattox. "History of Angelina County." Ancestry.com. M.A. Thesis, University of Texas. Austin, Texas. August 1937.

40 ibid.

41 Kennedy, Betty. Interview 170d. By R.L Kuykendall. Feb. 2002. Diboll History Center.

42 Kennedy, Betty. Interview 170a. By R.L Kuykendall. 12 Sep. 2002. Diboll History Center.

43 Boon, Effie Mattox. "History of Angelina County." Ancestry.com. M.A. Thesis, University of Texas. Austin, Texas. August 1937.
44 Bowman, Bob. "Nazis in East Texas." East Texas Historical Society, 1 January 2005.
45 ibid.
46 ibid.
47 Bowman, Bob. "Nazis in East Texas." East Texas Historical Society, 1 January 2005.
48 Diamond, Christina S. "Former POW Camp in Lufkin to be Dedicated Wednesday.." The Lufkin Daily News. 10 February 2007.
49 ibid.
50 ibid.
51 Negro Chamber of Commerce and Dunbar High School, Lufkin, Texas."The Mirror 1955-1956." Published by Collegiate Press. Kansas City, Mo.
52 Kennedy, Betty. Interview 170a. By R.L Kuykendall. 12 Sep. 2002. Diboll History Center.
 Kennedy, Betty. Interview 170b. By R.L Kuykendall. 12 Sep. 2002. Diboll History Center.
53 Kennedy, Betty. Interview 170a. By R.L Kuykendall. 12 Sep. 2002. Diboll History Center.
54 ibid.
55 Kennedy, Betty. Interview 170c. By R.L Kuykendall. Oct. 2002. Diboll History Center.
56 ibid.
57 Carrington, Sr. Ellis. Interview 244a. By R.L Kuykendall. 15 and 29 Jul 2002. Diboll History Center.
58 ibid.
59 ibid.
60 Kennedy, Betty. Interview 170c. By R.L Kuykendall. Oct. 2002. Diboll History Center.
61 ibid.
62 Kennedy, Betty. Interview 170d. By R.L Kuykendall. Feb. 2002. Diboll History Center.
63 Rhodes, Odis O. Interview 232b. By R.L Kuykendall. 2001. Diboll History Center.
64 Negro Chamber of Commerce and Dunbar High School, Lufkin, Texas."The Mirror 1955-1956." Published by Collegiate Press. Kansas City, Mo.
65 Rhodes, Odis O. Interview 232b. By R.L Kuykendall. 2001. Diboll History Center.
66 ibid.

[67] Carrington Sr, Ellis. Interview 244a. By R.L Kuykendall. 15 and July 29, 2002. Diboll History Center.

[68] Negro Chamber of Commerce and Dunbar High School, Lufkin, Texas."The Mirror 1955-1956." Published by Collegiate Press. Kansas City, Mo.

[69] ibid.

[70] Kennedy, Betty. Interview 170d. By R.L Kuykendall. Feb. 2002. Diboll History Center.

[71] The Bough. Diboll History Center, Diboll, Texas. Vol. 15, Dec. 2010

[72] Abstract of titled and patented lands compiled from the records of the Texas.,no. 436, To Lots (3) and (4) of the Chapman Addition to city of Lufkin, 16 May 1958.

[73] The Bough. Diboll History Center, Diboll, Texas. Vol. 15, Dec. 2010

[74] Coate, Duane. "Lufkin Dunbar High School." East Texas History, esttexashistory.org/items/show/335, Accessed 18 August 2021.

[75] Rhodes, Odis O. Interview 232b. By R.L Kuykendall. 2001. Diboll History Center.

[76] (61) Dunbar, Paul Laurence. "Lyrics of Lowly Life." Lit2Go Edition. 1913. etc.usf.edu/lit2go/187/lyrics-of-lowly-life. Accessed 26 February 2019.

[77] Coate, Duane. "Lufkin Dunbar High School." East Texas History, esttexashistory.org/items/show/335, Accessed 18 August 2021.

[78] ibid.

[79] "The Dunbar Tiger." Pictorial Edition. Vol. 2, No. 2, November 1943.

[80] Carrington Sr, Ellis. Interview 244a. By R.L Kuykendall. 15 and July 29, 2002. Diboll History Center.

[81] ibid.

[82] Rhodes, Odis O. Interview 232a. By R.L Kuykendall. 10Jan 2001. Diboll History Center.

[83] ibid.

[84] Boon, Effie Mattox. "History of Angelina County." Ancestry.com. M.A. Thesis, University of Texas. Austin, Texas. August 1937.

[85] Coate, Duane. "Lufkin Dunbar High School." East Texas History, esttexashistory.org/items/show/335, Accessed 18 August 2021.

[86] Rhodes, Odis O. Interview 232b. By R.L Kuykendall. 2001. Diboll History Center.

[87] (41) Dunbar High School Students. Interview 250a. By Angelina County Historical Commissions 6 October 2006. Diboll History Center.

[88] Coate, Duane. "Lufkin Dunbar High School." East Texas History, esttexashistory.org/items/show/335, Accessed 18 August 2021.

[89] Carrington Sr, Ellis. Interview 244a. By R.L Kuykendall. 15 and July 29, 2002. Diboll History Center.

90   Coate, Duane. "Lufkin Dunbar High School." East Texas History, esttexashistory.org/items/show/335, Accessed 18 August 2021.
91   ibid.
92   (41) Dunbar High School Students. Interview 250a. By Angelina County Historical Commissions 6 October 2006. Diboll History Center.
93   Coate, Duane. "Lufkin Dunbar High School." East Texas History, esttexashistory.org/items/show/335, Accessed 18 August 2021.
94   ibid.
95   ibid.
96   Carrington Sr, Ellis. Interview 244a. By R.L Kuykendall. 15 and July 29, 2002. Diboll History Center.
97   Coate, Duane. "Lufkin Dunbar High School." East Texas History, esttexashistory.org/items/show/335, Accessed 18 August 2021.
98   ibid.
99   ibid.
100   (55) Prairie View Interscholastic League, University Interscholastic League, uiltexas.org/history/psil. Accessed 7 Mar 2014.
101   (55)ibid.
102   (41) Dunbar High School Students. Interview 250a. By Angelina County Historical Commissions 6 October 2006. Diboll History Center.
103   , Bronwyn Turner. "Historical Panel Remembers Cotton Club," 10 Jan 2006. Lufkin Daily News
104   Bronwyn Turner. "Historical Panel Remembers Cotton Club," 10 Jan 2006. Lufkin Daily News
105   ibid.
106   Carrington Sr, Ellis. Interview 244a. By R.L Kuykendall. 15 and July 29, 2002. Diboll History Center.
107   Bronwyn Turner. "Historical Panel Remembers Cotton Club," 10 Jan 2006. Lufkin Daily News,
108   Rhodes, Odis O. Interview 232a. By R.L Kuykendall. 10Jan 2001. Diboll History Center.,
109   (54) "Zoot Suit Riots." History.com Editors. HISTORY. www.history.com/topics/world-war-ii/zoot-suit-riots. Access date: 23 Feb 2019.
110   Carrington Sr, Ellis. Interview 244a. By R.L Kuykendall. 15 and July 29, 2002. Diboll History Center.
111   Bronwyn Turner. "Historical Panel Remembers Cotton Club," 10 Jan 2006. Lufkin Daily News,
112   "T Bone Walker." Wikipedia.org. En-wikipedia.org/wiki/t-bone-walker. Web 31 May 2020.
113   Bronwyn Turner. "Historical Panel Remembers Cotton Club," 10 Jan 2006. Lufkin Daily News,

114   Carrington, Sr. Ellis. Interview 244a. By R.L Kuykendall. 15 and 29 Jul 2002. Diboll History Center.

115   (20) Abstract of titled and patented lands compiled from the records of the Texas.,no. 436, To Lots (3) and (4) of the Chapman Addition to city of Lufkin, 16 May 1958.

116   Aldon S. Lang and Christopher Long, "Land Grants," Handbook of Texas Online, accessed December 27, 2015, https://www.tshaonline.org/handbook/entries/land-grants.Published by the Texas State Historical Association.

117   Raymond Estep, "Zavala, Lorenzo de," Handbook of Texas Online, accessed 27, December 2015, https://www.tshaonline.org/handbook/entries/zavala-lorenzo-de.

118   Andreas V. Reichstein, "Galveston Bay and Texas Land Company," Handbook of Texas Online, accessed August 16, 2021, tshaonline.org/handbook/entries/galveston-bay-and-texas-land-company.Published by the Texas State Historical Association.

119 Land Grant Results, General Land Office and Court of Claims, State of Texas. File number SC 000055:37, Grantee: Quinalty, John Lewis. Deed of Sale, 27 April 1835, 1 League, Angelina County.

120   George Cook to Henry Raquet Plat, 7 August 1858. Montana Lillie original deed abstract of titled and patented lands compiled from the records of Texas., no. 436, To Lots (3) and (4) of the Chapman Addition to the city of Lufkin, 16 May 1958.

121   Kennedy, Betty. Interview 170a. By R.L Kuykendall. 12 Sep. 2002. Diboll History Center.

122   Aldon S. Lang and Christopher Long, "Land Grants," Handbook of Texas Online, accessed December 27, 2015, https://www.tshaonline.org/handbook/entries/land-grants.Published by the Texas State Historical Association.

123   Raymond Estep, "Zavala, Lorenzo de," Handbook of Texas Online, accessed 27, December 2015, https://www.tshaonline.org/handbook/entries/zavala-lorenzo-de.

124   Raymond Estep, "Zavala, Lorenzo de," Handbook of Texas Online, accessed 27, December 2015, https://www.tshaonline.org/handbook/entries/zavala-lorenzo-de.

125   Portrait of Major Henry W. Raguet, 4th Texas Mounted Rifles, Confederate States Army." Degolyer Library, Southern Methodist University - Law, Lawrence T. Jones III Collection. Accessed: 30 June 20 2018.

126   "Portrait of Major Henry W. Raguet, 4th Texas Mounted Rifles, Confederate States Army." Degolyer Library, Southern Methodist University - Law, Lawrence T. Jones III Collection. Accessed: 30 June 20 2018.

Bibliography References

Aldon S. Lang and Christopher Long, "Land Grants," *Handbook of Texas Online*, accessed December 27, 2015,

Andreas V. Reichstein, "Galveston Bay and Texas Land Company," *Handbook of Texas Online*, accessed August 16, 2021, tshaonline.org/handbook/entries/galveston-bay-and-texas-land-company.Published by the Texas State Historical Association.

Aragorn Storm Miller, "Raguet, Henry Wynkoop," *Handbook of Texas Online*, accessed August 16, 2021, tshaonline.org/handbook/entries/raguet-henry-wynkoop. Published by the Texas State Historical Association.

Berger, Maurice. "An unidentified couple." RACE STORIES, Documenting the Dynamic Black Community of 1940s Seattle. Al Smith Collection, MOHA. *NY Times*. Circa 1944. Published March 27, 2018. nytimes.com/2018/03/27/lens/ documenting-the-dynamic-black- community-of-1940s-seattle.html. Accessed 26 February 2019.

Biesele, Megan. "Angelina County." *Handbook of Texas Online.* Accessed 2 June 2020, tshaonline.org/handbook/entries/angelina. Published by the Texas State Historical Association.

Boon, Effie Mattox. "History of Angelina County." *Ancestry.com.* M.A. Thesis, University of Texas. Austin, Texas. August 1937.

Bowman, Bob & Doris. "The Forgotten Towns of East Texas.", *Best of East Texas Publishers*. Vol. 1.

Bowman, Bob. "Nazis in East Texas." *East Texas Historical Society*, 1 January 2005.

Bronwyn Turner. "Historical Panel Remembers Cotton Club," 10 Jan 2006. *Lufkin Daily News*.

Carrington Sr., Ellis. Interview 244a. By R.L Kuykendall. 15 and July 29, 2002. Diboll History Center.

Carrington, Sr. Ellis. Interview 244a. By R.L Kuykendall. 15 and 29 Jul 2002. Diboll History Center.

Coate, Duane. "Lufkin Dunbar High School." East Texas History, esttexashistory.org/items/show/335, Accessed 18 August 2021.

Cushman, Will. "Five Foundry Workers." Wisconsin Historical Society. 14 February 2020. wiscontext.org/great-migration-and-benoits-african-american-heritage. Accessed: 1 August 2021

Delano, Jack. "Caboose.", Library of Congress Prints and Photographs Division Washington, D.C. 20540 USA. 16 September 2009.

Dunbar High School Students. Interview 250a. By Angelina County Historical Commissions 6 October 2006. Diboll History Center.

Dunbar, Paul Laurence. "Lyrics of Lowly Life." Lit2Go Edition. 1913. etc.usf.edu/lit2go/187/lyrics-of-lowly-life. Accessed 26 February 2019.

East Texas Historical Association. *East Texas Historical Association Journal*. Vol. II, no.2, 1964, pg. 30.

Eugene C. Barker, "Mexican Colonization Laws," *Handbook of Texas Online*. Published by the Texas State Historical Association. Accessed August 16, 2021, tshaonline.org/handbook/entries/mexican-colonization-laws.

George Cook to Henry Raquet Plat, 7 August 1858. Montana Lillie's original deed.Abstract of titled and patented lands compiled from the records of Texas., no. 436, To Lots (3) and (4) of the Chapman Addition to the city of Lufkin, 16 May 1958.

Gottlieb, William P. "Dancers in a Jazz Club." *Library of Congress, Washington, DC.* Circa 1917. hdl.loc.gov/loc.pnp/pp.print. Web accessed, 29 May 2020.

Green, James R. "The Brotherhood of Timber Workers 1910-1913: A Radical Response to Industrial Capitalism in the Southern USA." The Past and Present Society. *Oxford University Press*. No. 6 (August 1973). pp. 161-200.

Haltom, R.W. "History and Description of Angelina County, Texas." *The Pemperton Press, Jenkins Publishing Company.* Austin, New York. October 1888.

History - Brown v. Board of Education. United States Courts. uscourts.gov/educational-resources. Accessed 15 Dec 2018.

History.com Editors. "Zoot Suit Riots." *HISTORY*. www.history.com/topics/world-war-ii/zoot-suit-riots. Access date: 23 Feb 2019.

https://www.tshaonline.org/handbook/entries/land-grants.*Published by the Texas State Historical Association.*

Kennedy, Betty. Interview 170a. By R.L Kuykendall. 12 Sep. 2002. Diboll History Center.

Kennedy, Betty. Interview 170b. By R.L Kuykendall. 12 Sep. 2002. Diboll History Center.

Kennedy, Betty. Interview 170c. By R.L Kuykendall. Oct. 2002. Diboll History Center.

Kennedy, Betty. Interview 170d. By R.L Kuykendall. Feb. 2002. Diboll History Center.

Land Grant Results, General Land Office and Court of Claims, State of Texas. File number SC 000055:37, Grantee: Quinalty, John Lewis. Deed of Sale, 27 April 1835, 1 League, Angelina County.

Lillie, Montana. 1930 U.S. Census, Lufkin, Angelina County, Tx. Roll 2288, pg. 4A, ED0001, Fig. 2342022, Web Accessed, 1 March 2014.

Lilly, Rosie. Interview 242a. By R.L Kuykendall. 26 Sep. 1988. Diboll History Center.

Map of Lufkin, Angelina County, *Texas.Sanborn Fire Insurance Company.* May 1922. loc.gov/iterm/sanborn08629_004.

Mark, Lottie K. Interview 239a. By R.L Kuykendall. 18 Sep. 2002. Diboll History Center.

Payne, Charles, Green, Adam, editors. Time Longer Than Rope.

Prairie View Interscholastic League, University Interscholastic League, uiltexas.org/history/psil. Accessed 7 March 2014.

Rhodes, Odis O. Interview 232a. By R.L Kuykendall. 10Jan 2001. Diboll History Center.

Rhodes, Odis O. Interview 232b. By R.L Kuykendall. 2001. Diboll History Center.

Texan Found Not Guilty, 1 April 1942. *The Vernon Daily Record., Newspaper.com.* Web 2 accessed: June 2020.

The Bough. Diboll History Center, Diboll, Texas. Vol. 15, Dec. 2010.

ToledobendLake.com, toledo-bend.com/attractions/sawmill. Web Accessed 17Feb2019.

Wikipedia contributors. "Natchitoches, Louisiana." Wikipedia, The Free Encyclopedia. *Wikipedia, The Free Encyclopedia,* 6 Aug. 2021. Web accessed: 16 Aug. 2021.

Wolcott, Marion Post. "One of tenant families on their porch, Marcella Plantation, Mississippi Delta, Mississippi." Oct.? 1939. *Library of Congress.* locn.gov/item/2017754632. WebAccessed 1 Jul 2020.

Wooster, Ralph A. "Life in Civil War East Texas." *East Texas Historical Society Journal.* Vol. III, no. 3, October 1965, pg. 93.

Figures and Tables Bibliography

Fig.   1   Adams, Andy. "Lufkin Civil rights Leader Rev. Betty Kennedy passes away at age 84." Lufkin Daily News, 25 July 2015.

Fig.   2   Diboll History Center. Diboll, Texas. @2022 Google map data. Web accessed 10 March 2022.

Fig.   3   "Montana Lille." c. 1965. Price, Ron. Family photograph collection.

Fig.   4   "Emma and Montana Lille." c. 1952. Price, Ron. Family photograph collection.

Fig.   5   "Map of Camp Creek in Union Parish, LA." Louisiana. Hometown Locator.com. louisiana.HometownLocator.com/maps/feature-map,ftc,54450. Web Accessed 13 October 2015.

Fig.   6   Map of Sabine Parrish Google map data © 2015, Web accessed: 15 December 2015.

Fig.   7   Stokes, George Alvin. "A Study of the Industry As a Culturo-Geographic Factor Lumbering in Southwest Louisiana." A Dissertation. Louisiana State University, May 1954, pg. 26.

Fig.   8   "Commissary . Logs hauled by teams by the Fisher Sawmill Days, Fisher, Louisiana." Sabine Parish Library.

Fig.   9   Johnston, Frances. "African American Guiding Log from Water onto Sawmill Ramp), Library of Congress. Washington, DC. Circa. 1899. loc.getarchive.net/media/african-american-guiding-log. Web Accessed: 5 December 2015.

Fig.   10   Fricker, Donna. "The Louisiana Lumber Boom, c.1880-1925", Historic Preservation Services LLC. National Archives and Records Great Lakes Region (Chicago). Published 1970. pg. 27.

Fig.   11   Typical Sawmill Worker Houses in Bogalusa, LA.

Fig.   12   National Archives and Records Great Lakes Region

<table>
<tr><td>Fig.</td><td>13</td><td>Ham, Debra Newman Editor. "Series: The African-American Mosaic:" A Library of Congress Resource Guide for the Study of Black History and Culture, Library of Congress, Pittsburgh, Pennsylvania 15250-7954, Stock number S/N 030-000-00254-7. Web Accessed 15 June 2021.</td></tr>
<tr><td>Fig.</td><td>14</td><td>"H.E.&W. Texas RR Depot." Luftex.com. Web accessed 19 February 2022.</td></tr>
<tr><td>Fig.</td><td>15</td><td>"City of Lufkin." c.1930-1960. c. 1965. Price, Ron. Family photograph collection.</td></tr>
<tr><td>Fig.</td><td>16</td><td>Bowman, Bob Editor."You'll Love Lufkin."City of Lufkin.com, cityoflufkin.com/history.htm. Web Accessed 11 July 2010.</td></tr>
<tr><td>Fig.</td><td>17</td><td>"First Street." c. 2006s. Price, Ron. Family photograph collection.</td></tr>
<tr><td>Fig.</td><td>18</td><td>Lomax, Ruby. "Angelina Four of Kelty's Lumber Co., Lufkin, Texas." Circa. Oct 1940. Library of Congress, Washington, D.C. lccn.loc.gov/2007660036. Web accessed: 19 January 2021.</td></tr>
<tr><td>Fig.</td><td>19</td><td>"Hoe Culture in the South. Negro Farmland." Library of Congress Prints and Photographs Division Washington, D.C. 20540 USA, locn.loc.gov/2017762955. Web accessed: 30 May 2020.</td></tr>
<tr><td>Fig.</td><td>20</td><td>"Angelina Hardwood Lumber." Luftex.com. Web Accessed: 19 February 2022.</td></tr>
<tr><td>Fig.</td><td>21</td><td>"Black Historic District." c.1930-1960. Price, Ron. Original map using approximate site locations mentioned throughout the book. Sites placed on maps by Google map data.</td></tr>
<tr><td>Fig.</td><td>22</td><td>"Brookshire Brothers." c. 1921. Countyline Magazine. <countylinemagazine.com/destination-guide/Lufkin/ brookshire-brothers-started-in-lufkin> Web accessed: 19 February 2022.</td></tr>
<tr><td>Fig.</td><td>23</td><td>Wiseman, H. O. "Harry Abram, " Texas Jewish Historical Society Records, di_10421, The Dolph Briscoe Center for American History, The University of Texas at Austin. "Harry Abram." Texas Jewish Historical Society.</td></tr>
</table>

Fig.   24   "So-called Shotgun Houses." Price, Ron. Family photograph collection

Fig.   25   "Portion of Third Ward of Houston, Texas." Wikimedia Commons. Circa 2017. Commons.wkimedia.org/wiki/File: thirdwardshotgunshacks.jpg. Web accessed: 1 June 2021.

Fig.   26   "Downtown c.1930-1960." Price, Ron. Original map using approximate site locations mentioned throughout the book. Sites placed on maps by Google map data.

Fig.   27   "Fire Station and City Hall." c. 1921. Bowman, Bob Editor. "The Lufkin That Was (A Centennial Album 1882-1982)." Lufkin Printing Company, Lufkin, Texas.

Fig.   28   "Negroes Working on the Railroad." Iowa.gov. iowaculture.gov/sites/default/files/primary-sources/Fig.s/history-educationpss-afamcivil-railroad-source.jpg. Web Accessed: 4 Aug 2021.

Fig.   29   History.com Editors. "Jim Crow Mandated Segregation." History.com. history.com/topics/early-20th-century-us/jim-crow-laws. Web Accessed: 1 June 2021.

Fig.   30   Downtown Lufkin. C. 1950. Luftex.com. Web accessed: 15 December 2020.

Fig.   31   "A Pullman Porter Makes Down A Sleeping Berth." National Museum of American History. Ids.si.edu/ids/deliveryservice?&id=NMAH-AC0181-0000001. Web Accessed: 11 September 2021.

Fig.   32   Kornweibel Jr, Theodore. "Railroads in the African American Experience: A Photographic Journey." Washington Book Publishers, Washington, D.C. Web Accessed: 26 February 2010.

Fig.   33   Dr. Percy Simond c. 1955. Negro Chamber of Commerce and Dunbar High School, Lufkin, Texas. "The Mirror 1955-1956." Published by Collegiate Press. Kansas City, Mo.

Fig.	34	"Site of Former Lufkin Land and Lumber." @2022 Google Maps, Web accessed: 1 March 2022.

Fig.	35	Typical East Texas Sawmill. C. 1910. Center for American History. UT—Austin, East Texas Photographic Collection (DI #01287).

Fig.	36	"Ties Awaiting Creosote Treatment." Wikipedia. commons.wikimedia.org/wiki/file:photograph-of-ties-awaiting-creosote-treatment-NARA_2129633.jpg.

Fig.	37	"Lufkin Land." c.1930-1960. Price, Ron. Original map using approximate site locations mentioned throughout the book. Sites placed on maps by Google map data.

Fig.	38	Diamond, Christina S. "Former POW Camp in Lufkin to be Dedicated Wednesday." The Lufkin Daily News. 10 February 2007.

Fig.	39	"World War II Soldiers with Captured Nazi Flag." Accession number 72-3951. Taken March 1, 1945. Courtesy of Harry S. Truman Library & Museum. Independence, MO.

Fig.	40	"Rothammer." Diamond, Christina S. "Former POW Camp in Lufkin to be Dedicated Wednesday." The Lufkin Daily News. 10 February 2007.

Fig.	41	"Negro Beauty Shops." Negro Chamber of Commerce and Dunbar High School, Lufkin, Texas. "The Mirror 1955-1956." Published by Collegiate Press. Kansas City, Mo.

Fig.	42	Smith Beauty Shop c.1956. Negro Chamber of Commerce and Dunbar High School, Lufkin, Texas. "The Mirror 1955-1956." Published by Collegiate Press. Kansas City, Mo.

Fig.	43	Houston Tatum Cleaners c. 1956. Negro Chamber of Commerce and Dunbar High School, Lufkin, Texas. "The Mirror 1955-1956." Published by Collegiate Press. Kansas City, Mo.

Fig.   44   Wolcott, Marion Post. "Haircutting in Front of General Store and Post Office on Marcella Plantation, Mississippi Delta, Mississippi." Circa 1939. Wikipedia. https://commons.wikimedia.org/wiki/File:Haircutting_in_Front_of_General_Store_and_Post_Office_on_Marcella_Plantation,_Mileston,_Mississippi_-_MET_1987.1100.260.jpg. Web Accessed: 1 July 2020.

Fig.   45   "Local Negro Businesses." Negro Chamber of Commerce and Dunbar High School, Lufkin, Texas."The Mirror 1955-1956." Published by Collegiate Press. Kansas City, Mo.

Fig.   46   Roe, Ken. "Lynn Theatre." Cinema Treasures, cinematreasures.org/theaters/20363. Accessed 11 July 2010.

Fig.   47   Feller, Patrick. "Pines Theatre in Lufkin, Texas." Published 24 Nov 2011. Commons.wikimedia.org. flickr.com/photos/nakrnsm/6405534583.

Fig.   48   "Tims Funeral Home." Negro Chamber of Commerce and Dunbar High School, Lufkin, Texas."The Mirror 1955-1956." Published by Collegiate Press. Kansas City, Mo.

Fig.   49   "Colonial Mortuary." Negro Chamber of Commerce and Dunbar High School, Lufkin, Texas."The Mirror 1955-1956." Published by Collegiate Press. Kansas City, Mo.

Fig.   50   "Lewis Service Station and Malone Barbershop." Negro Chamber of Commerce and Dunbar High School, Lufkin, Texas. "The Mirror 1955-1956." Published by Collegiate Press. Kansas City, Mo.

Fig.   51   "Finus Price, First Negro Blacksmith Shop." Price, Ron. Family photograph collection.

Fig.   52   "Typical Blacksmith Shop." Johnston, Frances. "The Village Smith" circa 1906. Reproduction: Library of Congress, Washington, DC. loc.gov/pictures/item/90710736. Web accessed: 31 May 2020.

Fig.   53   "Typical Cotton Gin Equipment." The African Americans: Many Rivers to Cross, video. The WNET Group. Web accessed: 19 February 2022.

Fig.   54   "Downtown." c. 1930-1960. Price, Ron. Original map using approximate site locations mentioned throughout the book. Sites placed on maps by Google map data.

Fig.   55   "Angelina Hotel & Coffee Shop." C. 1920s. Luftex.com. Web accessed: 19 February 2022.

Fig.   56   "King Faisal II touring a cotton-gin plant." Accession Number 72-684, Circa. August 1952. Courtesy of Harry S. Truman Library & Museum. Independence, MO.

Fig.   57   "North Addition." c.1930-1960. Price, Ron. Original map using approximate site locations mentioned throughout the book. Sites placed on maps by Google map data.

Fig.   58   Charlie Williams Yankees. C. 1956.Negro Chamber of Commerce and Dunbar High School, Lufkin, Texas. "The Mirror 1955-1956." Published by Collegiate Press. Kansas City, Mo.

Fig.   59   "Lewis Motel & Beauty Shop." Negro Chamber of Commerce and Dunbar High School, Lufkin, Texas."The Mirror 1955-1956." Published by Collegiate Press. Kansas City, Mo.

Fig.   60   Carl Williams Youth baseball, c. 1956. Negro Chamber of Commerce and Dunbar High School, Lufkin, Texas. "The Mirror 1955-1956." Published by Collegiate Press. Kansas City, Mo.

Fig.   61   "James Hackney Grocery Store." Negro Chamber of Commerce and Dunbar High School, Lufkin, Texas. "The Mirror 1955-1956." Published by Collegiate Press. Kansas City, Mo.

Fig.   62   "James Hackney." Negro Chamber of Commerce and Dunbar High School, Lufkin, Texas. "The Mirror 1955-1956." Published by Collegiate Press. Kansas City, Mo.

Fig.   63   "How African American Visitors Found Texas BBQ During the Jim Crow Era." Circa 1947. Vaughn, Daniel. Texas Monthly. texasmonthly.com/bbq/green-book-barbeque/. Web Accessed: 11 September 2021.

Fig.   64   "Dr. Samuel C. Packer." Negro Chamber of Commerce and Dunbar High School, Lufkin, Texas. "The Mirror 1955-1956." Published by Collegiate Press. Kansas City, Mo.

Fig.   65   "Sheppard's BBQ." Negro Chamber of Commerce and Dunbar High School, Lufkin, Texas. "The Mirror 1955-1956." Published by Collegiate Press. Kansas City, Mo.

Fig.   66   "Martin's Dental Clinic." Negro Chamber of Commerce and Dunbar High School, Lufkin, Texas." The Mirror 1955-1956." Published by Collegiate Press. Kansas City, Mo.

Fig.   67   "Ida V. Givens." Negro Chamber of Commerce and Dunbar High School, Lufkin, Texas."The Mirror 1955-1956." Published by Collegiate Press. Kansas City, Mo.

Fig.   68   "House's Café." Negro Chamber of Commerce and Dunbar High School, Lufkin, Texas."The Mirror 1955-1956." Published by Collegiate Press. Kansas City, Mo.

Fig.   69   "William & Son Grocery." Negro Chamber of Commerce and Dunbar High School, Lufkin, Texas."The Mirror 1955-1956." Published by Collegiate Press. Kansas City, Mo.

Fig.   70   "East Texas Undertaking." Negro Chamber of Commerce and Dunbar High School, Lufkin, Texas. "The Mirror 1955-1956." Published by Collegiate Press. Kansas City, Mo.

Fig.   71   "Inez Tims." Negro Chamber of Commerce and Dunbar High School, Lufkin, Texas. "The Mirror 1955-1956." Published by Collegiate Press. Kansas City, Mo.

Fig.   72   "Slim Jenkins Garage." Negro Chamber of Commerce and Dunbar High School, Lufkin, Texas. "The Mirror 1955-1956." Published by Collegiate Press. Kansas City, Mo.

Fig.   73   "Gulf Service Station." Negro Chamber of Commerce
                and Dunbar High School, Lufkin, Texas. "The Mirror
                1955-1956." Published by Collegiate Press. Kansas
                City, Mo.

Fig.   74   "Geneva's Drive-in." Negro Chamber of Commerce
                and Dunbar High School, Lufkin, Texas. "The Mirror
                1955-1956." Published by Collegiate Press. Kansas
                City, Mo.

Fig.   75   "Universal Life." Negro Chamber of Commerce and
                Dunbar High School, Lufkin, Texas. "The Mirror 1955-
                1956." Published by Collegiate Press. Kansas City, Mo.

Fig.   76   "Lufkin Foundry." Negro Chamber of Commerce and
                Dunbar High School, Lufkin, Texas. "The Mirror 1955-
                1956." Published by Collegiate Press. Kansas City, Mo.

Fig.   77   "Texas Foundry." Negro Chamber of Commerce and
                Dunbar High School, Lufkin, Texas. "The Mirror 1955-
                1956." Published by Collegiate Press. Kansas City, Mo.

Fig.   78   "Texas Foundry Employees." Negro Chamber of
                Commerce and Dunbar High School, Lufkin, Texas.
                "The Mirror 1955-1956." Published by Collegiate
                Press. Kansas City, Mo.

Fig.   79   "Negro, Texas Foundry Employees Being Served." c.
                1955. Price, Ron. Personal collection.

Fig.   80   "Southland Papermill." Negro Chamber of Commerce
                and Dunbar High School, Lufkin, Texas. "The Mirror
                1955-1956." Published by Collegiate Press. Kansas
                City, Mo.

Fig.   81   "New Zion Baptist Church." c. 1920s. Negro Chamber
                of Commerce and Dunbar High School, Lufkin, Texas.
                "The Mirror 1955-1956." Published by Collegiate
                Press. Kansas City, Mo.

Fig.   82   "New Zion Baptist Church." c. 1940s. Negro Chamber
                of Commerce and Dunbar High School, Lufkin, Texas.
                "The Mirror 1955-1956." Published by Collegiate
                Press. Kansas City, Mo.

Fig.   83   "Goodwill Baptist Church." C. 1900. Negro Chamber of
Commerce and Dunbar High School, Lufkin, Texas.
"The Mirror 1955-1956." Published by Collegiate
Press. Kansas City, Mo.

Fig.   84   "Goodwill Baptist Church (new)." C. 1921. Negro
Chamber of Commerce and Dunbar High School,
Lufkin, Texas."The Mirror 1955-1956." Published by
Collegiate Press. Kansas City, Mo.

Fig.   85   "First Baptist Church." c.1921. Negro Chamber of
Commerce and Dunbar High School, Lufkin, Texas."The
Mirror 1955-1956." Published by Collegiate Press.
Kansas City, Mo.

Fig.   86   "Mt. Calvary Baptist Church." Negro Chamber of
Commerce and Dunbar High School, Lufkin, Texas."The
Mirror 1955-1956." Published by Collegiate Press.
Kansas City, Mo.

Fig.   87   "Shiloh Baptist Church." Negro Chamber of Commerce
and Dunbar High School, Lufkin, Texas. "The Mirror
1955-1956." Published by Collegiate Press. Kansas
City, Mo.

Fig.   88   "Long Chapel C.M.E. Church." Negro Chamber of
Commerce and Dunbar High School, Lufkin, Texas.
"The Mirror 1955-1956." Published by Collegiate
Press. Kansas City, Mo.

Fig.   89   "West End Church of God in Christ." Negro Chamber
of Commerce and Dunbar High School, Lufkin, Texas.
"The Mirror 1955-1956." Published by Collegiate
Press. Kansas City, Mo.

Fig.   90   "Other Lufkin Area Negro Churches." Negro Chamber
of Commerce and Dunbar High School, Lufkin, Texas.
"The Mirror 1955-1956." Published by Collegiate
Press. Kansas City, Mo.

Fig.   91   "Other Lufkin Area Negro Churches continued." Negro
Chamber of Commerce and Dunbar High School,
Lufkin, Texas. "The Mirror 1955-1956." Published by
Collegiate Press. Kansas City, Mo.

Fig.   92   "Lufkin, Texas." c.1930-1960. Price, Ron. Original map
using approximate site locations mentioned

throughout the book. Sites placed on maps by Google map data.

Fig.   93   "G.W. Carver Elementary." Tatum, Marva E. Editor. "Tiger '64." Dunbar High School Annual, Taylor Publishing Co.

Fig.   94   Third Grade Carver Elementary c. 1956

Fig.   95   "Olivia R. Hackney." Tatum, Marva E. Editor. "Tiger '64." Dunbar High School Annual, Taylor Publishing Co.

Fig.   96   "Brandon Elementary." Tatum, Marva E. Editor. "Tiger '64." Dunbar High School Annual, Taylor Publishing Co.

Fig.   97   "Original Garrett Elementary." Tatum, Marva E. Editor. "Tiger '64." Dunbar High School Annual, Taylor Publishing Co.

Fig.   98   "Melinda Garrett." Tatum, Marva E. Editor. "Tiger '64." Dunbar High School Annual, Taylor Publishing Co.

Fig.   99   Third Grade Carver Elementary c. 1956

Fig.   100   "Newer Garrett Elementary." Tatum, Marva E. Editor. "Tiger '64." Dunbar High School Annual, Taylor Publishing Co.

Fig.   101   "Cedar Grove Elementary." Tatum, Marva E. Editor. "Tiger '64." Dunbar High School Annual, Taylor Publishing Co.

Fig.   102   "Lucky Ward," c. 1920s. Courtesy Museum of East Texas. Lufkin, Texas.

Fig.   103   "Lucky Ward Graduating Class." c. 1920s. Courtesy Museum of East Texas. Lufkin, Texas.

Fig.   104   "Lucky Ward Faculty," c. 1920s. Museum of East Texas. Lufkin, Texas.

Fig.   105   "Dunbar High School." Negro Chamber of Commerce and Dunbar High School, Lufkin, Texas." The Mirror 1955-1956." Published by Collegiate Press. Kansas City, Mo.

Fig.   106   "William Brandon," c. 1956. Negro Chamber of Commerce and Dunbar High School, Lufkin, Texas. "The Mirror 1955-1956." Published by Collegiate Press. Kansas City, Mo.

Fig.   107   "Dunbar High School Faculty." c. 1934. Pictorial Edition. Vol. 2, No. 2, November 1943.

Fig.   108   "F.W. Thomas Dunbar Principal 1943-44." The Dunbar Tiger. Pictorial Edition. Vol. 2, No. 2, November 1943.

Fig.   109   "W.R. Smith Dunbar Football Coach." The Dunbar Tiger. Pictorial Edition. Vol. 2, No. 2, November 1943.

Fig.   110   "Dunbar District Champions, 1943-44." The Dunbar Tiger. Pictorial Edition. Vol. 2, No. 2, November 1943.

Fig.   111   "Dunbar Football Team, 1939." Negro Chamber of Commerce and Dunbar High School, Lufkin, Texas. "The Mirror 1955-1956." Published by Collegiate Press. Kansas City, Mo.

Fig.   112   "Dunbar Pep Squad Leaders 1943-44." The Dunbar Tiger. Pictorial Edition. Vol. 2, No. 2, November 1943.

Fig.   113   "Typical Flatbed Truck." c. 1930. Courtesy - Kim Loeb Collection - Kenworth Trucks, https://www.google.com/ search?hl=en&sxsrf= ALeKk01sPvmFuvVgwnWOk6UYH1R2_nvkMQ:162904 5398911&q=kim+loeb+collection&tbm=isch&chips=q: kim+loeb+collection,online_chips:kenworth+truck:tGK rwi0Yz4k%3D&usg=AI4_&biw=1366&bih=625. Web accessed: Dec. 2015.

Fig.   114   "Dunbar Basketball Team of 1938." Negro Chamber of Commerce and Dunbar High School, Lufkin, Texas. "The Mirror 1955-1956." Published by Collegiate Press. Kansas City, Mo.

Fig.   115   "Dunbar Leadership 1943-44." The Dunbar Tiger. Pictorial Edition. Vol. 2, No. 2, November 1943.

Fig.   116   "Miss Dunbar 1943-44." The Dunbar Tiger. Pictorial Edition. Vol. 2, No. 2, November 1943.

Fig.   117   "Dunbar High School Band," c.1956. Negro Chamber of Commerce and Dunbar High School, Lufkin, Texas. "The Mirror 1955-1956." Published by Collegiate Press. Kansas City, Mo.

Fig.   118   "English Department." Tatum, Marva E. Editor. "Tiger '64." c. 1964. Dunbar High School Annual, Taylor Publishing Co.

Fig.   119   "M.E. Lyons Dunbar Principal." The Dunbar Tiger.
                 Pictorial Edition. Vol. 2, No. 2, November 1943.

Fig.   120   "Student Safety Patrol," c.1956. Negro Chamber of
                 Commerce and Dunbar High School, Lufkin, Texas.
                 "The Mirror 1955-1956." Published by Collegiate
                 Press. Kansas City, Mo.

         121   "New Dunbar High School," c. 1952. Tatum, Marva E.
                 Editor. "Tiger '64." c. 1964. Dunbar High School
                 Annual, Taylor Publishing Co.

Fig.   122   "Dunbar Football Coaching Staff." Tatum, Marva E.
                 Editor. "Tiger '64." c. 1964. Dunbar High School
                 Annual, Taylor Publishing Co.

Fig.   123   "1930 Track Team," c. 1956. Negro Chamber of
                 Commerce and Dunbar High School, Lufkin, Texas.
                 "The Mirror 1955-1956." Published by Collegiate
                 Press. Kansas City, Mo.

Fig.   124   "Varsity Football Team." Tatum, Marva E. Editor.
                 "Tiger '64." c. 1964. Dunbar High School Annual, Taylor
                 Publishing Co.

Fig.   125   "Dunbar Tennis Team." Tatum, Marva E. Editor. "Tiger
                 '64." c. 1964. Dunbar High School Annual, Taylor
                 Publishing Co.

Fig.   126   "Girls' Track Team." Tatum, Marva E. Editor. "Tiger
                 '64." c. 1964. Dunbar High School Annual, Taylor
                 Publishing Co.

Fig.   127   "Girls' Track Team," c.1956. Negro Chamber of
                 Commerce and Dunbar High School, Lufkin, Texas.
                 "The Mirror 1955-1956." Published by Collegiate
                 Press. Kansas City, Mo.

Fig.   128   "Domestic Engineers." Tatum, Marva E. Editor. "Tiger
                 '64." c. 1964. Dunbar High School Annual, Taylor
                 Publishing Co.

Fig.   129   "Miss Dunbar." Tatum, Marva E. Editor. "Tiger '64." c.
                 1964. Dunbar High School Annual, Taylor Publishing
                 Co.

Fig.   130   "Lufkin Dunbar Jr. High," Tatum, Marva E. Editor.
                 "Tiger '64." c. 1964. Dunbar High School Annual, Taylor
                 Publishing Co.

Fig.   131   "Dunbar Library." Negro Chamber of Commerce and Dunbar High School, Lufkin, Texas. "The Mirror 1955-1956." Published by Collegiate Press. Kansas City, Mo.

Fig.   132   "North Addition." c.1930-1960. Price, Ron. Original map using approximate site locations mentioned throughout the book. Sites placed on maps by Google map data.

Fig.   133   "Square Deal Taxi Stan," c.1956. Negro Chamber of Commerce and Dunbar High School, Lufkin, Texas. "The Mirror 1955-1956." Published by Collegiate Press. Kansas City, Mo.

Fig.   134   Alford, Holly. "The Zoot Suit: Its History and Influence." Fashion Theory. The Journal of Dress, Body & Culture. no. 2 (2004): 225. Accessed 3 May 2012.

Fig.   135   "Ray Charles." Circa. 15 July 2003. Wikimedia Commons. Commons.wikimedia.org/wiki/file: ray_charles_ FIJM_2003.jpg.Web: 1 June 2020.

Fig.   136   Thornton, Cedric. "Little Richard." Arts and Culture Lifestyle News. 9 May 2020. blackenterprise.com/little-richard-rock-and-roll-pioneer-dead-at-87. Accessed 24 Jul 2021.

Fig.   137   Smith, John Matthew. "B.B. King." Published 14 Dec 2018. Commons.wikimedia.org. flickr.com/photos/ kingphoto/ 46264650642.

Fig.   138   "Duke Ellington." Biograph, biography.com/people/ duke-ellington. Accessed 24 Jul 2021.

Fig.   139   Author unknown. "Fats Domino. "Wikimedia Commons. Circa 1956. Commons.wkimedia.org/wiki/ file:fats_domingo-1956_png. Web 1 June 2020. Web 1 June 2020.

Fig.   140   "T Bone Walker." Wikipedia.org. En-wikipedia.org/ wiki/t-bone-walker. Web:31 May 2020.

Fig.   141   "Sammy Davis Jr." Wikimedia Commons. Circa 1972. Commons.wkimedia.org/wiki/File: Sammy Davis jr. 1972 jpg. Web: 1 June 2020.

Fig.   142   Author unknown. "Ike and Tina Turner." Wikimedia Commons. Circa 1973. Commons.wkimedia.org/wiki/file: -Ike-&-Tina-Turner-Midnight-Special-1974_jpg. Web: 1 June 2020.

Fig.   143   "Ethel Waters." Wikimedia Commons. Circa 1943. Commons.wkimedia.org/wiki/File: Ethel Waters-1943 jpg. Web: 1 June 2020.

Fig.   144   "Otis Redding." Wikimedia Commons. Circa 1967. Commons.wkimedia.org/wiki/File: Waters-1943 jpg. Web: 1 June 2020.

Fig.   145   "Black Historic District." c. 1930-1960. Price, Ron. Original map using approximate site locations mentioned throughout the book. Sites placed on maps by Google map data.

Fig.   146   "Montana Lille Home." c. 2006. Price, Ron. Family photograph collection.

Fig.   147   "Lucky Ward Deeded Plat." c. 1965. Price, Ron. Family photograph collection.

Fig.   148   "Outhouse." Free Stock Photos. stockvault.net/free-photos/outhouse. Accessed 28 May 2020.

Fig.   149   "Vintage Galvanized Wash Tub." Worthpoint.com. worthpoint.com/worthopedia/vintage-wash-tub-bin-1826134624. Accessed 22 July 2021.

Fig.   150   428/430 Chestnut c. 1970, Author's family home.

Fig.   151   Lange, Dorothea. "The Cotton Sharecropper's Unit is One Mule and the Land He Can Cultivate with a One-Horse Plow." Library of Congress, Washington DC. Circa. 1937. hdl.loc.gov/loc.pnp/pp.print.Web 28 May 2020.

Fig.   152   "African American Woman Doing Laundry with a Scrub Board and Tub." Library of Congress, Washington, DC. hdl.loc.gov/loc.pnp/cph.3a51106. Web 22 May 2020.

Fig.   153   Keipp, Mary Morgan. "Churning Butter." Encyclopedia of Alabama, Courtesy of the Selma Depot Museum. Encyclopediaofalabama.org/article/m-2043. Accessed 8 September 2015.

Fig.   154   "1956 Studebacker." Smartmotorguide.com. smartmotorguide.com. studebacker-president-original-cars-for-sale-in Florida. Accessed Dec 2015.

Fig.   155   "Montana Lille Gravesite." c. 2006. Price, Ron. Family photograph collection.

Fig.   156   "Emma Lille Gravesite." c. 2006. Price, Ron. Family photograph collection.

Fig.   157   Perry, Mike. "The White Dove As A Messenger Of The Dead." 67. Not Out. 67notout.com/2012/02/white-dove-as-messenger-of-dead.html. Accessed: 23 Feb 2019.

Fig.   158   "Emma Lillie." c. 1950s. Price, Ron. Family photograph collection.

Fig.   159   "Bobby Jindal." Wikipedia Commons. Wikipedia.org/wiki/Bobby Jindal. Accessed 19 Feb 2019.

Fig.   160   "L.C. Lille." c. 1970s. Price, Ron. Family photograph collection.

Fig.   161   "Patricia Lillie McKenzie." c. 1960s. Price, Ron. Family photograph collection.

Fig.   162   "Clark Jackson Price." c. 1948. Price, Ron. Family photograph collection.

Fig.   163   "Vera Lillie." c. 1940s. Price, Ron. Family photograph collection.

Fig.   164   Raymond Estep, "Zavala, Lorenzo de." Handbook of Texas Online. https://www.tshaonline.org/ handbook/ entries/zavala-lorenzo-de. Web accessed: accessed 27 December 2015.

Fig.   165   "Portrait of Major Henry W. Raguet, 4th Texas Mounted Rifles, Confederate States Army." Degolyer Library, Southern Methodist University - Law, Lawrence T. Jones III Collection. Web Accessed: 30 June 20, 2018.

Table 1. "City of Lufkin." C. 1930-1960. . Price, Ron Legend, with additional location information and comments to accompany maps prepared by the author

Table 2. "Downtown." c. 1930-1960. Price, Ron Legend, with additional location information and comments to accompany maps prepared by the author.

Table 3. "Lufkin Land." c. 1930-1960. Price, Ron. Legend with additional location information and comments to accompany maps prepared by the author.

Table 4. "Downtown." c. 1930-1960. Price, Ron. Legend with additional location information and comments to accompany maps prepared by the author.

Table 5. "North Addition." c. 1930-1960. Price, Ron. Legend with additional location information and comments to accompany maps prepared by the author.

Table 6. "North Addition." c. 1930-1960. Price, Ron. Legend with additional location information and comments to accompany maps prepared by the author.

Table 7. Abstract of titled and patented lands compiled from the records of the Texas. No. 436, Two Lots (3) and (4) of the Chapman Addition to city of Lufkin, 16 May 1958.

Author's Page

Ron Price is a self-published author. His books can be purchased directly from Amazon.com

His current published works are:

World Sports Guide - Illustrated introduction to the most popular global sports
Rise of Women's Basketball - Follows a fictional college Women's Basketball team before Title IX
Education of a Black Man - Life of G.H. Fortner: Soldier, preacher, scholar and community activist
Family Life in Slavery - Historical fiction of life in slavery for one family as they struggle to survive together
Healthy Habits for Superhero Kids - Children's Picture book on keeping safe during these challenging times
Kindergarten Detective - Children's Picture book that follows a 5-year old as she solves a great mystery
Magic Drum - Children's Picture book that retells a famous African folktale

Visit his author's page at
https://amazon.com/author/ronpricebooks

Index

Black Business

Atlanta Life Insurance, 79

Beauty Rest Barber Shop, 55

Colonial Mortuary, 62

Dodd's Barber Shop, 55

Doris' Beauty Shops, 55

Dr. Packard's Clinic, 21, 71, 146

Dr. Simmons' Clinic, 25, 73, 113

Geneva's Drive-In, 50, 71, 84, 120, 146

Gulf Service Station, 70, 83, 145

House's Cafe, 58, 80

Ingram, Will - Architect, 21, 22, 25, 27, 43, 54, 97, 98, 158

James Hackney Grocery Store, 75

James Mattox Gulf Service Station, 58

Lewis Motel, 73

Lewis Service Station, 61

Malone's Barber Shop, 55

Martin's Dental Clinic, 79

McGruder Barber Shop, 55

Papy Dad's Bar B-Q, 58

Sheppard's BBQ, 78

Slim Jenkins' Garage, 58, 83

Taylor's Beauty Shop, 58

Tims Funeral Home, 60, 82

Universal Life Insurance, 84

William & Son Grocery, 81

Black Developments

Jack Stroud Quarters, 21, 125

Joe's Quarters, 21, 25, 71, 146

Nesbitt Quarters, 21

Walker Quarters, 29, 35, 67, 70, 145

Black Residential Areas

Downtown, 26, 34, 35, 36, 38, 39, 54, 59, 63, 64, 65, 66, 67, 68, 216

Historical District, 24, 25, 26, 75, 113, 157, 158

Lufkin Land, 45, 46, 47, 48, 54, 98, 216

North Addition, 33, 69, 70, 144, 146, 216

Blacksmith, 35, 54, 63, 64, 66, 91

Brakemen, 41, 148

Chestnut Street, 25, 26, 27, 30, 42, 73, 75, 76, 98, 101, 108, 113, 158, 159, 160, 161, 163, 165, 168, 173, 175, 180

Churches

First Baptist, 21, 42, 70, 98, 124, 145

Goodwill, 21, 25, 43, 97, 98

Long Chapel, 21, 25, 101

Mt. Calvary, 99

New Zion, 37, 42, 43, 70, 95, 96, 145, 175

Shiloh, 70, 100, 145

Cotton Gin, 35, 64, 66, 68

Dance Clubs

Blue Room for Teenagers, 25, 73, 180

Clyde Davis Night Club, 70, 145

Congo Club, 29, 70, 71, 145, 146

Cotton Club, 41, 70, 145, 147, 148, 149, 155, 193, 196

McClendon's Clubs, 48, 70, 155

Pine Grove Dance Hall, 70, 145

Dunbar High School

Band, 130, 131, 133

Basketball, 124, 129, 217

C.L. Franklin, 125

Coach Elmer Redd, 135, 136

Develous Johnson, 125

Football, 125, 126, 127, 135, 136, 138, 169

Learning, 120, 122, 133

School Supplies, xii, 120, 122, 217

Sports Recognition, 136, 137, 138, 139, 140

Grade Schools

Brandon Elementary, 70, 100, 109, 118, 120, 134, 145

Carver Elementary, 25, 48, 107, 108

Cedar Grove Elementary, 21, 112

Garrett Elementary, 71, 110, 112, 113, 117, 120, 131, 133, 135, 139, 146

Jones Park, 32, 70, 145

Lille, Emma

Big Mamma, 171

Birthplace, 180

churning butter, 31, 169

Culinary Skills, 169

Soap Versatility, 32, 165, 167, 170

Washtub, 163, 167

Lille, Montana

Cause of death, 175

Favorite weapon, 31, 158, 173, 174

Known as Mountain Man, xvi, 168, 175

Love of pinto beans, 171

Many, LA, xvi, 1, 2, 9, 10, 11, 22, 31, 33, 38, 47, 78, 90, 172, 180

Working in the sawmills, 7, 9, 10, 16, 45, 46, 47, 49, 87, 92, 93, 199

Lucky Ward Colored School

Faculty, 116

Graduates, 115

History, 113, 117, 118, 122

Location, 114, 161, 183

Major Employers

Lufkin Foundry, 35, 40, 66, 87, 88

Southland Paper Mill, 49, 51, 92, 93

Texas Foundry, 40, 88, 89, 90, 91, 92, 182

Medicine

Access to Medical care, 45, 73, 77, 78, 158

Dr. McClendon, 73
Dr. Samuel C. Packard, 77
Dr. Simmons, 25, 73, 113
Movie Theatres
  Lynne, 35, 59, 66
  Pine, 36, 67, 70, 145
  Texan, 35, 59, 66, 172, 199
Nazi Prison Camp, 49, 51, 52
Negro Bus. Dist.
  One Thousand, 68
Obstacles

Curfew, 36
Jim Crow Laws, 38, 53
Segregation, 37, 38, 53, 155
Price, Finus Blacksmith, 63, 91
Sawmill commissary, 16, 45, 47
Texas History
  Land Grants, 160, 183, 187
  Lorenzo de Zavala, 184
  Quintalty Land, 183, 187
Zoot suits, 149, 150, 193, 197